People and Religion
in North America

People and Religion in North America

Summaries of Biographical Articles in History Journals

People in History Series

Pamela R. Byrne and
Susan K. Kinnell, Editors

ABC-CLIO

Santa Barbara, California
Oxford, England

Cover design by Tanya Nigh
Book design by Susan K. Kinnell

Library of Congress Cataloging in Publication Data

People and religion in North America.

    (The People in history series)
    Includes indexes.
    1. Religious biography—United States.
2. Religious biography—Canada. I. Byrne, Pamela R.
II. Kinnell, Susan K. III. Series.
BL2525.P46 1988   291'.092'2 [B]   88-6227
ISBN 0-87436-542-2

10 9 8 7 6 5 4 3 2 1

ABC-Clio, Inc.
2040 Alameda Padre Serra, Box 4397
Santa Barbara, California 93103

Clio Press Ltd.
55 St. Thomas Street
Oxford, OX1 1JG, England

CONTENTS

Preface vii

Summaries of Biographical Articles 1

Subject Index 119

Author Index 163

List of Periodicals 167

PREFACE

This is a book about people who participated in the religious life of North America. Not every religious leader that you can think of is in this book, nor is every important detail of the person's life mentioned. PEOPLE AND RELIGION IN NORTH AMERICA has 364 biographical summaries of articles about US and Canadian people involved in all phases of the religious life of America. Entries include coverage of articles about missionaries, preachers, educators, and other people of various faiths including Catholics, Jews, Protestants, Mormons, and Quakers as well as some lesser-known religious sects.

Using this volume, students can select topics for term papers and identify the names of a specific person they wish to research further. Fictional or composite characters can be created by reading about several people of the same faith or living in a particular time and place. Role enactment in the classroom will be greatly enhanced by access to the people described in these summaries. Students' understanding of history can broaden as they begin to understand the role that religious experiences played in the formation of America. A number of the summaries cover the lives of people who dedicated themselves to issues of church and state, religious liberty, and education.

PEOPLE AND RELIGION IN NORTH AMERICA differs from a standard biographical dictionary that provides short, structured paragraphs about well-known people. Instead, this book brings to the reader's attention lesser-known people in addition to a sampling of religious leaders. The chronological scope of the summaries ranges from the seventeenth century to the present, and the lives touched upon are those of people who have been the subjects of historians' research in the many journals covered in *AMERICA:HISTORY AND LIFE*. The stories of these people will give a sense of the richness and diversity of everyday life at various times, providing a dimension to the study of history that is not often found in textbooks.

The entries in this book are summaries of some of the articles that have appeared over the years in thousands of history journals and selected by the editors at ABC-CLIO. It is to be hoped that the inclusion of varying sources (the journal literature from which these articles and summaries were taken) will help point students in the direction of new avenues of research and help them consider new sources of information that are outside the realm of their usual classroom and library study. The list of journals covered in this book contains a number of titles that will be familiar to secondary school teachers and librarians and several that they may not previously have considered as a source for curriculum research. Interlibrary loans should provide access to these more unfamiliar journals so that further exploration and research may be carried out.

A NOTE ON HOW TO USE THIS BOOK:

The summaries are arranged alphabetically by name, with a list of the article authors, and the periodicals covered. There is a detailed subject index that will allow the student to find people by region, religious faith or sect, ethnic origin, or other unique factors. See the note at the beginning of the index for a discussion on how to use this index. All summaries and their original articles are in English. If there is more than one article about a person, the articles are arranged under each name alphabetically by the author of the article. If the original article had no author, the article is listed with the title first. A sample entry follows on the next page.

SAMPLE ENTRY

Name of Person

BUTLER, PIERCE

Entry Number

Article Author

35. Noonan, John T., Jr. THE CATHOLIC
JUSTICES OF THE UNITED STATES
SUPREME COURT.

Article Title

Catholic Hist. Rev. 1981 67(3): 369-385.

Journal Information

Discusses five Catholic justices of the United
States Supreme Court: Roger Brooke Taney
(1777-1864), Edward Douglas White (1845-
1921), Joseph McKenna (1843-1926), Pierce
Butler (1866-1939), and Frank Murphy (1890-
1949). The article looks at the points where their
Catholicism had an impact upon their careers in
terms of their appointments or their judicial
actions and the points where, conversely, their
careers had an impact on the Catholic Church.

Summary

PEOPLE AND RELIGION IN NORTH AMERICA

A

AITKEN, ROGER

1. Dunlop, A. C. A HOUSE IS NOT A HOME—REV. ROGER AITKEN AND THE STRUGGLE FOR A LUNENBURG RECTORY. *Collections of the Royal Nova Scotia Hist. Soc. (Canada) 1982 41: 47-63.*

Reverend Roger Aitken spent the last years of his life as an Episcopal clergyman in Lunenburg, one of eight missions in Nova Scotia sponsored by the Society for the Propagation of the Gospel in Foreign Parts. His sojourn as rector of St. John's Anglican Church, Lunenburg, was one of the most tumultuous in the history of the congregation, with the congregation splitting over the issue of the rectory in the Wentzell House. Aitken showed "determination and dedication" not only in the rectory issue, but in his very active involvement in such community affairs as schools and road-building.

ANCKER, HENRIETTA

2. Stern, Norton B. THE CHARITABLE JEWISH LADIES OF SAN BERNARDINO AND THEIR WOMAN OF VALOR, HENRIETTA ANCKER. *Western States Jewish Hist. Q. 1981 13(4): 369-376.*

Henrietta Ancker (1835-90) came to San Bernardino, California, with her husband Louis in 1870. She was very active in social and charitable activities, and in 1886 she helped organize the Ladies' Hebrew Benevolent Society. In tribute to her energetic leadership, the members changed the name to the Henrietta Hebrew Benevolent Society in 1891.

ANDERSON, DAVID

3. Peake, F. A. DAVID ANDERSON: THE FIRST LORD
BISHOP OF RUPERT'S LAND.
J. of the Can. Church Hist. Soc. (Canada) 1982 24(1): 3-46.

David Anderson became the first lord bishop of the bishopric of
Rupert's Land in 1849. According to the Church Missionary
Society in England, his episcopal duties were to train the Indians
to be ministers and to translate the Bible into their tongues. His
relations with the Hudson's Bay Company, upon whom he
depended for all his material needs, were strained. While he
encouraged an agricultural life for the Indians, the company's
profits demanded that they remain nomadic hunters and
fishermen. Anderson also experienced strained relations with his
poorly selected and undertrained clergy and with Presbyterians.
He returned to England in 1865.

ANDERSON, GEORGE EDWARD

4. Francis, Rell G. VIEWS OF MORMON COUNTRY: THE
LIFE AND PHOTOGRAPHS OF GEORGE EDWARD
ANDERSON.
Am. West 1978 15(6): 14-29.

At the age of 17, after serving as an apprentice where he
mastered the principles and techniques of photography, Mormon
George Edward (George Ed) Anderson (1860-1928) set up
business for himself. He was quick to adopt new ideas and to
devise such things as portable studios. He traveled throughout
southern Utah to remote villages, mining camps, or wherever
opportunity for people-centered civic activities, rural industry,
and community celebrations beckoned. About two-thirds of his
some 40,000 photographs were studio portraits. He was also
motivated by an insatiable quest to document Mormon Church
history and subjects. Anderson's work has been featured in
several publications and in recent exhibits.

ASHLEY, JONATHAN

5. Coughlin, Robert C. JONATHAN ASHLEY: TORY
MINISTER.
Hist. J. of Western Massachusetts 1979 7(2): 35-40.

Jonathan Ashley, minister of Deerfield, was one of a number of Massachusetts ministers whose support for the King caused serious conflicts for them with their congregations. As the dispute between the colonies and the mother country intensified, he found himself cut off from his flock. The town expressed its displeasure with his views by cutting off his supply of firewood during the winter as an alternative to removing him. When Ashley died in 1780 the conflict had not been resolved.

B

BACKUS, ISAAC

6. Grenz, Stanley J. ISAAC BACKUS AND THE ENGLISH BAPTIST TRADITION.
Baptist Q. (Great Britain) 1984 30(5): 221-231.

Gives an account of Isaac Backus's involvement with the Separate Baptists of New England, emphasizing his encouragement of close ties between English and American Baptists; organizer and pastor of the Baptist church in Middleborough, Massachusetts, Backus has been called the "Father of American Baptists."

BACON, THOMAS

7. Deibert, William E. THOMAS BACON, COLONIAL CLERGYMAN.
Maryland Hist. Mag. 1978 73(1): 79-86.

Surveys the American career of the Anglican priest Thomas Bacon (1700-68), rector of St. Peter's Parish, Talbot County, Maryland, and after 1758 of All Saints Church in Frederick. Though he was fundamentalist and conservative in religious and political beliefs, Bacon's ministry had a progressive social content, and he not only preached that slaves should be taught Christianity but also founded perhaps the first charity working school in Maryland. His project of publishing the laws of Maryland flung him into a four-year political battle (centered on inclusion or omission of the 1661 Tonnage Act) between the proprietary and antiproprietary parties in the General Assembly.

Minister, musician, physician, educator, gardener, and student of law, he exemplified the 18th-century Renaissance man and achieved a prominence matched by few Maryland clergymen.

BAKER, GEORGE (FATHER DIVINE)

8. Pearson, Fred Lamar, Jr. and Tomberlin, Joseph Aaron. JOHN DOE, ALIAS GOD: A NOTE ON FATHER DIVINE'S GEORGIA CAREER.
Georgia Hist. Q. 1976 60(1): 43-48.

George Baker (later, "Father Divine") was born in Savannah and grew up in the South. He became involved with Samuel Morris, "Father Jehovia," in Baltimore and assumed the title "The Messenger." The trinity was completed with the addition of St. John the Vine Hickerson. There was soon to be conflict over divinity, and Hickerson and "The Messenger" moved in independent directions. Baker went to Valdosta where he began to develop a following, mainly of black females. Eventually (1914) he was taken to court, and after a series of court battles, he was acquitted and left Valdosta with some of his followers.

BALDASSARRE, RAFFAELE

9. Baldassarre, Raffaele; Troy, Ferdinand M., ed., transl.; Steele, Thomas J., transl. FATHER BALDASSARRE WRITES HOME.
Colorado Coll. Studies 1982 (19): 187-191.

Raffaele Baldassarre wrote a letter in Italian to friends in Italy describing daily life and religious customs in the Jesuit parish in Conejos, Colorado, which was published in *Lettere Edificanti dei Padri della Compagnia di Gesu della Provincia Napoletana* (Edifying letters of the fathers of the Naples Province of the Society of Jesus), vol. 1 (1874), pp. 82-84. Ferdinand M. Troy (Trojanek) translated it into Latin and added comments in his undated typescript, "Historica Societatis Jesu in Novo Mexico et Colorado" (History of the Society of Jesus in New Mexico and Colorado), Regis Jesuit History Library, Denver. Prints an English translation of Troy's Latin compared with the Italian original.

BARR, D. EGLINTON

10. Fowler, Arlen L. CHAPLAIN D. EGLINTON BARR: A LINCOLN YANKEE.
Hist. Mag. of the Protestant Episcopal Church 1976 45(4): 435-438.

When the Civil War began, Northern-born D. Eglinton Barr was rector of St. John's Episcopal Church, Baton Rouge, Louisiana. Because of his Northern heritage, he was suspect in the eyes of the Confederates. He went to the Federal lines in New Orleans, volunteered as a Chaplain, and was assigned to the 81st Regiment of US Colored Troops. Later he was apprehended and imprisoned by Confederates, but escaped and returned to New Orleans. At the end of the war, with former Confederates returning to power he was not allowed employment. He thus returned to the Army chaplaincy, was again assigned to a black regiment, and conducted school for his troops until he retired in 1872. The Department of Education of Texas presented him with a letter of appreciation for his work in the field of public education. His story provides an insight into the human side of times and events that are often forgotten.

BARTOL, CYRUS

11. Heath, William G., Jr. CYRUS BARTOL'S TRANSCENDENTAL CAPITALISM.
Studies in the Am. Renaissance 1979: 399-408.

Cyrus Bartol, minister of the Unitarian West Church in Boston, was a familiar figure in the religious, intellectual, and literary life of New England during the 19th century. He was, however, besides a religious figure, also a shrewd businessman, and had no rival "in combining the dual roles of seer and doer." Bartol became acquainted with Manchester-by-the-Sea in Massachusetts in the 1850's, and made his first important real estate purchase in 1871. Over the next quarter century Bartol bought, improved, and sold additional properties in Manchester. His business investments were to him for spiritual benefit. He used his investments as a means of putting into practice some of his strongest religious beliefs. He conceived nature as chaotic and in need of improvement by man. It is not hard to see a connection between this idea and his tremendous effect on the development of Manchester.

BATES, ELISHA

12. Good, Donald G. ELISHA BATES AND THE HICKSITE CONTROVERSY.
Quaker Hist. 1981 70(2): 104-117.

According to Elisha Bates, an evangelical Quaker in Mount Pleasant, Ohio, Christianity was divided into denominations, differing in sacraments, ritual, and polity, but united on a creed including the divinity of Christ, His atonement to save sinners, and the authority of the Bible. In 1825 he had published extracts from the writings of early Friends and an exposition of Quaker doctrine. In 1827 he founded the *Miscellaneous Repository* to defend orthodoxy against such Hicksites as William Gibbon, editor of the Wilmington, Delaware, *Berean*. Bates was prominent in the schism of Ohio Yearly Meeting precipitated by Elias Hicks's 1828 visit. Bates seemed to enjoy controversy and exaggerated his opponents' views.

GOOD, DONALD G.

13. ELISHA BATES AND THE BEACONITE CONTROVERSY.
Quaker Hist. 1984 73(1): 34-47.

In their evangelical publications against what they took to be the doctrines of Elias Hicks, Quakers Elisha Bates, of Mount Pleasant, Ohio, and Isaac Crewdson, of Manchester, England, based their arguments on the authority of the Bible. Crewdson's *A Beacon to the Society of Friends* (1835) led to controversy among English Quakers and the separation of the "Beaconites." Bates associated with Anna and Isaac Braithwaite, Beaconite sympathizers, on his two trips to England, 1833-36. His belief in the primacy of Scripture convinced him to be baptized with water, for which he was disowned by the Society of Friends in 1837.

BEACH, JOHN

14. Mappen, Marc. ANGLICAN HERESY IN EIGHTEENTH CENTURY CONNECTICUT: THE DISCIPLINING OF JOHN BEACH.
Hist. Mag. of the Protestant Episcopal Church 1979 48(4): 465-472.

The only colonial Connecticut Anglican clergyman ever charged with heresy, John Beach (1700-82), was a convert from Congregationalism. He rejected much of the theology of his former colleagues, and even wrote devastating pamphlets against them. In 1755, he published a book asserting that at the moment of death each individual comes into the presence of Christ and is judged then, rather than on Judgment Day. The Connecticut Congregational clergy, spotting this potential heresy, sent a copy of the work to Beach's ecclesiastical superiors in England. Reprimand followed. Beach backed down and went on to serve the Church, being the last Anglican parson in Connecticut to pray for the King's health.

BELKNAP, JEREMY

15. Kirsch, George B. JEREMY BELKNAP AND THE PROBLEM OF BLACKS AND INDIANS IN EARLY AMERICA.
Hist. New Hampshire 1979 34(3-4): 202-222.

Historian and Congregational minister Jeremy Belknap (1744-98) was one of the first analysts to think critically about a multiracial society in America. Although his upbringing often led him to judge nonwhites harshly if they deviated from his idea of proper personal conduct, he was more sympathetic to them than were most Americans. In his *History of New Hampshire* (1784, 1791-92), Belknap tried to be objective about Indians and their experiences with Europeans, although he became pessimistic about their future. Belknap wrote less about blacks than about Indians, but was an active opponent of slavery, and was hopeful about their future.

BENNARD, GEORGE

16. Pies, Frank John, Sr. and Pies, Timothy Mark. THE OLD RUGGED CROSS.
Michigan Hist. 1984 68(5): 36-39.

Methodist minister George Bennard authored over 350 religious songs, of which the most prominent was "The Old Rugged Cross." Bennard was born in Youngstown, Ohio, in 1873, but moved to Michigan in his adult life. The song brought fame and notoriety to Bennard, who traveled to 46 states to give lectures on the song's origin and to preach the gospel message. Through it all, Bennard retained a humble perspective and died quietly in Reed City, Michigan, in 1958.

BERGNER, PETER

17. Whyman, Henry C. PETER BERGNER, PIONEER MISSIONARY TO SWEDISH SEAMEN AND IMMIGRANTS.
Swedish Pioneer Hist. Q. 1979 30(2): 103-116.

Peter Bergner (1797-1866) and his family arrived in New York City in 1832 to settle there after Peter had led the sailor's life. He was converted to active Christianity in 1844 and began to preach to immigrant Swedes and Swedish sailors in their own language. These services were held on ships, or floating Bethels, under the auspices of the Methodist Church. This article is the story of Peter Bergner and also of these Bethel Ships. Peter Bergner died in 1866, having worked for the Lord for 17 years.

BIEN, HERMAN M.

18. Clar, Reva and Kramer, William M. JULIUS ECKMAN AND HERMAN BIEN: THE BATTLING RABBIS OF SAN FRANCISCO.
Western States Jewish Hist. Q. 1983 15(2): 107-130, (3): 232-253.

Part 1. Julius Eckman and Herman M. Bien were San Francisco's first two elected rabbis, and founders of the first two Jewish newspapers in the West. Eckman's mild nature was not suited for the contentious career of a rabbi, but his erudition served him well as publisher of the *Weekly Gleaner*, founded in January 1857. Bien's competing paper, *Voice of Israel,* founded three months earlier than the *Gleaner,* reflected the radical outlook of its publisher, and failed in April 1857. The bitter feud between the two rabbis was based in part on Bien's youth and his efforts to reform the services of Congregation Emanu-El, and on Eckman's attacks on Bien's qualifications. Part 2. In 1859, Eckman was joined by a young reporter, Isidor N. Choynski, who was later to become the leading Jewish journalist on the West Coast. The next year, Israel Joseph Benjamin, an international Jewish correspondent, toured the West, and his travels were fully reported in Eckman's *Weekly Gleaner.* The feud between Eckman and Bien cooled down while Bien successfully wrote and produced a play based on the story of Samson and Delilah.

19. Clar, Reva and Kramer, William M.   JULIUS ECKMAN AND HERMAN BIEN: THE BATTLING RABBIS OF SAN FRANCISCO.
Western States Jewish Hist. Q. 1983 15(4): 341-359.

Part 3. Continued from a previous article. In 1860-61, Herman Bien's weekly Jewish newspaper, *The Pacific Messenger,* failed. He then had a varied career for several years, running a general merchandise store in New York, and working on newspapers in Nevada Territory and New York City. In 1879, he went to Dallas as a rabbi; from 1881 to 1885 he was rabbi of Chicago's Congregation Beth Shalom. His final post was that of rabbi of Congregation Anshe Chesed in Vicksburg, Mississippi. Bien died by his own hand in 1895 after losing his Vicksburg rabbinate. Julius Eckman changed the name of his San Francisco paper to the *Hebrew Observer* in 1865, but resigned as editor several months later to resume religious duties.

BINGHAM, HIRAM

20. Miller, Char. THE MAKING OF A MISSIONARY: HIRAM BINGHAM'S ODYSSEY.
Hawaiian J. of Hist. 1979 13: 36-45.

Examines Hiram Bingham's early life in Vermont before he sailed for Hawaii in 1819. Age 21 was a turning point for Bingham (1789-1869), because at that time he was to become his parents' caretaker. Instead, he publicly took the vows of the

Lord. His conversion to Congregationalism gave him an excuse to break his commitment to his parents. This decision was due largely but not solely to his ambition. Bingham was raised in a religion that demanded intense commitment that went beyond family ties. The demands of his forceful and uncompromising personality fit the requirements of his missionary vocation.

21. Miller, Char, ed. "TEACH ME O MY GOD": THE JOURNAL OF HIRAM BINGHAM (1815-1816). *Vermont Hist. 1980 48(4): 225-235.*

At Middlebury College, 1813-16, Hiram Bingham groped toward a missionary career in the Sandwich Islands (Hawaii), 1819-39. At Andover Theological Seminary, 1816-18, he was active in the Tract Society. Bingham learned Hawaiian, opened Hawaiian schools, became influential with the royal family, and incurred the enmity of merchants and sailors for his Moral Wars on alcohol, prostitution, and gambling.

BINGHAM, HIRAM, III

22. Miller, Char. "THE WORLD CREEPS IN": HIRAM BINGHAM III AND THE DECLINE OF MISSIONARY FERVOR. *Hawaiian J. of Hist. 1981 15: 80-99.*

In choosing a secular over a religious career, Hiram Bingham III broke a long-standing family tradition of dedication to missionary life. In his youth, Bingham found his invalid parents' preoccupation with death, their rigid adherence to Congregational morality, and the idiosyncratic rituals repulsive. Changing values in the islands and a decline in missionary influence and power in the late 19th century influenced Bingham away from a religious career. Bingham's education at Phillips Academy and Yale finalized the break with his religious roots. Upon graduation, Bingham returned to Hawaii and briefly taught Bible school; however, he declined his parents' wish to pursue a missionary career in China. In 1899, Hiram, at age 24, sailed to San Francisco and began graduate work in history at the University of California at Berkeley.

BLAKE, ALICE

23. Foote, Cheryl J. ALICE BLAKE OF TREMENTINA: MISSION TEACHER OF THE SOUTHWEST. *J. of Presbyterian Hist. 1982 60(3): 228-242.*

Alice Blake was typical of devout American Presbyterian women who felt the call to take the civilizing aspects of the Protestant gospel to those who were under the iron hand of Romanism in the Southwest. Chronicles her labors, which culminated in the village of Trementina, New Mexico, where she labored for 30 years. In addition to being a teacher, she took the necessary courses that qualified her as a public health nurse, while at the same time she filled in from time to time as leader in worship when no minister was present. Protestant mission teachers like Blake came to the area laden with the sameattitudes of ethnic and cultural superiority that characterized their countrymen. But they also brought a firm and sincerecommitment to the Christian faith and a loving desire to serve.

BLAND, SALEM

24. Allen, Richard. SALEM BLAND: THE YOUNG PREACHER. *J. of the Can. Church Hist. Soc. (Canada) 1977 19(1-2): 75-93.*

After World War I, Salem Bland became recognized as a leader in the social gospel and liberal theology movements. The formative period for Bland was his early years as a Methodist minister in Canada. Though successful as a preacher, he held some suspect views and disliked the numerous theological controversies going on around him. Using his various talents, Bland sought to show that there was no important difference between science and religion and that Christian perfection meant not freedom from mistakes, but the constant desire to do what was right. Seeking at all times to combine the good from his own culture and fundamental Christian ideas, Bland rejected the evangelistic approach of both the Methodists and the Salvation Army because he felt that they could not help combine the old and the new.

BLIEMEL, EMMERAN

25. Meaney, Peter J. VALIANT CHAPLAIN OF THE BLOODY TENTH. *Tennessee Hist. Q. 1982 41(1): 37-47.*

Traces the career of Benedictine Father Emmeran Bliemel (1831-64), chaplain of the 10th Confederate Infantry and friend of the 4th Kentucky Regiment. The German-born Bliemel went from ordination in Pennsylvania to the diocese of Nashville, where he became attached to the Confederate cause. He died during the Battle of Jonesborough, Georgia, thus becoming the first Catholic chaplain to die in action serving his men.

BOTTOMS, LAWRENCE W.

26. Brackenridge, R. Douglas. LAWRENCE W. BOTTOMS: THE CHURCH, BLACK PRESBYTERIANS AND PERSONHOOD. *J. of Presbyterian Hist. 1978 56(1): 47-60.*

Interviews Lawrence Bottoms, first black Moderator of the Southern Presbyterian Church, and first black to head any major white Protestant denomination's black work. Traces Bottoms's life through his educational and pastoral career, giving insights into prejudice which confronted him. Out of such experiences his religious philosophy of personhood emerged. Bottoms strongly urged the Presbyterian Church in the South to reach out to the growing black middle class.

BOUCHER, JONATHAN

27. Clark, Michael D. JONATHAN BOUCHER AND THE TOLERATION OF ROMAN CATHOLICS IN MARYLAND. *Maryland Hist. Mag. 1976 71(2): 194-204.*

An Anglican minister of Queen Anne's Parish, Jonathan Boucher has been cited "as an exception to the almost universal anti-Catholicism of colonial Protestants, especially for his 1774 sermon "On the Toleration of Papists."' Others have noted his hypocrisy in holding out sympathy for Catholics only to enlist them in the Loyalist cause during the Revolution. Actually the more just verdict of him is "opportunism". A devotee of 18th-century paternalistic conservatism, with a "melioristic position," Boucher had an ecumenical disposition which urged the reunion of Catholic, Protestant Englishman, and Presbyterian, with the Anglican confession being the most fit "centre of union." Moreover, the collapse of Jacobitism after 1746 had removed much of the political rationale for Catholic-baiting. Though he urged freedom of religious conviction, Boucher remained fixed in his period's belief that such toleration did not extend to granting equality of political status to dissenters.

BRAINERD, DAVID

28. Conforti, Joseph. DAVID BRAINERD AND THE NINETEENTH CENTURY MISSIONARY MOVEMENT. *Journal of the Early Republic 1985 5(3): 309-329.*

Despite a tragically short life marked by illness, personal loss, and repeated disappointment, the Connecticut evangelical minister David Brainerd became a revered figure among early 19th-century evangelical missionaries. Thanks to Jonathan Edwards's extremely popular and highly romanticized *Life of Brainerd* (1748), Brainerd's meager missionary achievements took on heroic proportions. Missionary groups looking for a new role model found inspiration in Brainerd's work among Eastern Indian tribes and discovered the revivalist-pietist impact of the First Great Awakening. An outgrowth of Brainerd's popular appeal was the emphasis Edwards placed on disinterested benevolence and regeneration. Although disinterested benevolence fired missionary zeal, it could not overcome ethnocentrism and selfish attention to personal conversion. In Edwards's hands, Brainerd's life resembled a Puritan devotional work, and it provided a model for 19th-century missionary memoirs.

29. Conforti, Joseph. JONATHAN EDWARDS'S MOST POPULAR WORK: *THE LIFE OF DAVID BRAINERD* AND NINETEENTH-CENTURY EVANGELICAL CULTURE. *Church History 1985 54(2): 188-201.*

The life of David Brainerd (1718-47), notable for his missionary work among the Indians and for his expulsion from Yale because of his radical religious enthusiasm, was the subject of a 1749 work by Jonathan Edwards that became an evangelical classic. Edwards's *An Account of the Life of the Late Reverend*

Mr. David Brainerd became so influential in 19th-century evangelical culture because of its succinct presentation of a life representing true holiness and benevolence. It is through this work that Edwards most influenced 19th-century evangelical religious reform.

BROWN, VIOLET GOLDSMITH

30. Brown, Violet. OVER THE RED DEER: LIFE OF A HOMESTEAD MISSIONARY.
Alberta History (Canada) 1985 33(3): 9-18.

Violet Goldsmith Brown arrived in Saskatchewan in 1905, married the Reverend John Brown, who became a Presbyterian minister the next year, and spent the rest of her life as a homesteading missionary. Follows the family's travels and settlement in Saskatchewan, and finally near the Red Deer River in Alberta. Illness and debt plagued the Browns, but farming and hunting in the area provided a fresh food supply.

BROWNLOW, WILLIAM GANNAWAY

31. Conklin, Forrest. PARSON BROWNLOW JOINS THE SONS OF TEMPERANCE (PART I).
Tennessee Hist. Q. 1980 39(2): 178-194.

William Gannaway "Parson" Brownlow (1805-77) was a Methodist minister who became editor of *The Whig* (Knoxville) in 1838, and forsook his traveling ministry. At this time, efforts for greater liquor control were developing. One of the sources for temperance reform was the temperance societies. Brownlow carried on the fight for reform in the columns of his paper and in 1851 engaged in verbal debate over the issue. Largely material from the Knoxville and the Jonesboro *Whig;* 50 notes.

KELLY, JAMES C.

32. WILLIAM GANNAWAY BROWNLOW.
Tennessee Historical Quarterly 1984 43(1): 25-43, (2): 155-172.

Part 1. William Gannaway Brownlow was born in Virginia in 1805 and became a preacher after being deeply affected by a camp meeting in 1825. Brownlow proved "to have an unexcelled talent for ridicule and invective," and acquired "a reputation for pugnacity, eloquence, and ugliness." He became the first editor of the *Tennessee Whig* newspaper in 1839 and later moved his paper to Knoxville, where it became the *Knoxville Whig* and achieved a circulation that equalled all other East Tennessee newspapers combined. Brownlow became involved in state politics and engaged in "wholesale abuse of individuals in language of unparalleled severity." Although he was proslavery, he opposed secession. Part 2. Brownlow's *Whig* was the only newspaper in the Confederacy in June 1861 that opposed the existence of a Confederate government, and it met with broad support in East Tennessee, where most residents were opposed to the Confederacy. Making his way to federally controlled Nashville and later to Ohio, Brownlow became a celebrity and something of a hero. His 1862 book *Sketches of the Rise, Progress, and Decline of Secession,* later to become known simply as *Parson Brownlow's Book,* became a best-seller, and Brownlow toured the North making speeches of a patriotic nature. After the Civil War, Brownlow became governor of Tennessee, which embroiled him in Reconstruction politics, and later a United States senator.

BRUNSON, ALFRED

33. Schulte, Steven C. ALFRED BRUNSON AND THE WISCONSIN MISSIONARY FRONTIER. *Methodist Hist. 1981 19(4): 231-237.*

Alfred Brunson became a Methodist preacher in 1810. After serving in the War of 1812, he started to ride a circuit in western Pennylvania and Ohio. In 1835 he proposed that the church found an Indian mission in Wisconsin. Brunson accepted the invitation to become one of the missionaries. He helped in many ways to help build the American Methodist Church and to carry civilization into the wildernesses of the United States.

BURR, AARON

34. Geissler, Suzanne B. AARON BURR, JR.: DARLING OF THE PRESBYTERIANS.
J. of Presbyterian Hist. 1978 56(2): 134-147.

Although both his maternal grandfather (Jonathan Edwards) and his father (Aaron Burr, Sr.) had been presidents of the College of New Jersey (Princeton), and thus much was anticipated and expected of him, Aaron Burr, Jr. (1756-1836) never lived up to the hopes which his family and friends held out for him. His prestigious background made him "that darling of the Presbyterians." He was never able to be himself. His ancestry provided him with fame, connections, and a good many votes in the political arena and he ran for President in 1800; however it also provided him with a reputation impossible to live up to, dooming him to a lifetime of comparisons to his illustrious forebears.

BUTLER, PIERCE

35. Noonan, John T., Jr. THE CATHOLIC JUSTICES OF THE UNITED STATES SUPREME COURT.
Catholic Hist. Rev. 1981 67(3): 369-385.

Discusses five Catholic justices of the United States Supreme Court: Roger Brooke Taney (1777-1864), Edward Douglas White (1845-1921), Joseph McKenna (1843-1926), Pierce Butler (1866-1939), and Frank Murphy (1890-1949). The article looks at the points where their Catholicism had an impact upon their careers in terms of their appointments or their judicial actions and the points where, conversely, their careers had an impact on the Catholic Church.

BYINGTON, CYRUS

36. Coleman, Louis. CYRUS BYINGTON: MISSIONARY TO THE CHOCTAWS.
Chronicles of Oklahoma 1984-85 62(4): 360-387.

Despite his training as a lawyer, Cyrus Byington became a fervent missionary for the American Board of Commissioners for Foreign Missions during 1820. He first served the Choctaw

Indians at Mayhew Mission in central Mississippi, and then accompanied them to their new home in southeastern Oklahoma in 1835. In addition to ministering to the Indians, Byington wrote a Choctaw hymnal, grammar, and dictionary, all noted for their accuracy and comprehensiveness. His poor health and Choctaw factionalism during the Civil War troubled Byington's later years, but he remained at his post almost to the time of his death.

C

CABLE, GEORGE WASHINGTON

37. Farley, Benjamin W. GEORGE W. CABLE: PRESBYTERIAN ROMANCER, REFORMER, BIBLE TEACHER.
J. of Presbyterian Hist. 1980 58(2): 166-181.

In the last 25 years there have been three biographies of George Washington Cable (1844-1925), Southern Presbyterian, ex-Confederate soldier, and author of Creole stories. All three acknowledge his Presbyterian roots, and examine the influence of his church and home on his life and work. Concentrates attention on Cable as a Presbyterian, and explores his life, stories, and reforming activities in light of his Calvinistic heritage. Emphasizes the influence of his early home and training on his work and habits, the role of New Orleans Presbyterianism in his development, and, as his career advanced and his vision matured, how he drew upon and reacted against his Presbyterian heritage.

CAMERON, DONALDINA

38. McClain, Laurene Wu. DONALDINA CAMERON: A REAPPRAISAL.
Pacific Hist. 1983 27(3): 24-35.

Reviews Donaldina Cameron's career with the Presbyterian Mission Home in San Francisco and her efforts to save illegally imported Chinese women from the slave trade. Her attitude toward the women exhibited little tolerance or sympathy and hampered her attempts to rehabilitate them. Although she spent 40 years in Chinatown she did not speak Chinese and referred to the Chinese as heathens.

CANEVIN, JOHN F. REGIS

39. Schmandt, Raymond H. SOME NOTES ON BISHOP J. F. REGIS CANEVIN OF PITTSBURGH (1904-1921). *Records of the American Catholic Historical Society of Philadelphia 1984 95(1-4): 91-107.*

During John F. Regis Canevin's career as bishop of St. Paul's Cathedral in Pittsburgh, the diocese saw spectacular development, both physically and spiritually. Historians call the bishop "an astonishing man" because of his accomplishments, but since he avoided publicity, his personality has remained elusive. The warm, personal tone of a group of 96 extant letters between Canevin and his friend Lawrence Flick, collected at the Archives of the Catholic University of America, may help dispel Canevin's reputation as a cool, detached man. Reprints 16 Canevin-Flick letters, dated 1885 to 1921, with commentary.

CANNON, MARTHA HUGHES

40. Lieber, Constance L. "THE GOOSE HANGS HIGH": EXCERPTS FROM THE LETTERS OF MARTHA HUGHES CANNON. *Utah Hist. Q. 1980 48(1): 37-48.*

Martha Hughes Cannon (1857-1932) was the fourth polygamous wife of Angus Munn Cannon, president of the Salt Lake Stake of the Mormon Church. To prevent Angus Cannon's arrest for polygamy, Martha exiled herself to England during 1885-87. Her letters reveal loneliness, constant fear of exposure, fear of Cannon's arrest, and jealousy of other wives. The 1890 Manifesto allowed her to live openly in Salt Lake City and continue her medical career. In 1896 she became the first woman state senator in the United States.

CARTWRIGHT, PETER

41. Bray, Robert. BEATING THE DEVIL: LIFE AND ART IN PETER CARTWRIGHT'S AUTOBIOGRAPHY. *Illinois Historical Journal 1985 78(3): 179-194.*

The *Autobiography of Peter Cartwright,* the Backwoods Preacher (1856) sold over 30,000 copies in the United States and was equally successful when published in England three years later. It was the story of Peter Cartwright, a Methodist revivalist preacher. The autobiography was structured in terms of diametric oppositions: Cartwright as a Southern, Western, rural, masculine, and Methodist type versus the Yankee, Eastern, urban, feminine, and other religious types.

CARVER, WILLIAM OWEN

42. Dobbins, Gaines S. WILLIAM OWEN CARVER, MISSIONARY PATHFINDER. *Baptist Hist. and Heritage 1978 14(4): 2-6, 15.*

William Owen Carver (1868-1954), a professor at the Southern Baptist Theological Seminary, taught a "Comparative Religion and Missions" course, which emphasized the Bible's missionary message, and that every Christian should be committed to being a missionary. Carver's ideas represented the turning point in Baptist thought after 50 years of the "great split" between the pro-missionaries and the anti-missionaries.

CAVE, ROBERT CATLETT

43. Pearson, Samuel C., Jr. RATIONALIST IN AN AGE OF ENTHUSIASM: THE ANOMALOUS CAREER OF ROBERT CAVE. *Missouri Hist. Soc. Bull. 1979 35(2): 99-108.*

A theological liberal, Robert Catlett Cave (1843-1923) became pastor of the Central Christian Church at St. Louis in 1888. From that pulpit he challenged many traditional Christian views and was, as a consequence, ousted from his pastorate. Case and his followers then formed their own congregation and, for more than a decade, Cave remained on Protestantism's most "liberal fringe." Eventually he became an advocate of universalist theology based on nature and reason.

CHAMBERS, SAMUEL D.

44. SAINT WITHOUT PRIESTHOOD: THE COLLECTED TESTIMONIES OF EX-SLAVE SAMUEL D. CHAMBERS. *Dialogue 1979 12(2): 13-21.*

Samuel D. Chambers, long-time black member of the Church of Jesus Christ of Latter Day Saints, converted to Mormonism in 1844 while a slave youth, and though illiterate and soon isolated from other members of the faith, remained true to its teachings for 25 years, until circumstances permitted him to emigrate to Salt Lake City. He soon became a Deacon, but being black prohibited advancement to the priesthood. Contains publication of minutes of his testimonies during 1873-76, primarily consisting of thanks to God and the church for the good life he enjoyed.

CHANNING, WILLIAM ELLERY

45. McGuffie, Duncan S. WILLIAM ELLERY CHANNING'S RELIGION AND ITS INFLUENCE. *Tr. of the Unitarian Hist. Soc. (Great Britain) 1980 17(2): 45-53.*

A note on William Ellery Channing on the bicentennial of his birth describes Channing's religious convictions, including his reaction against Calvinism, and his early attempts to bridge the gulf between Unitarians and Trinitarians. Although he resisted the idea, there was a transcendental element in Channing's religious outlook. It stemmed from the Puritan tradition and 18th-century rationalism, and produced a belief of human perfectibility expressed in rational vocabulary.

CHINIQUY, CHARLES

46. Brettell, Caroline B. FROM CATHOLICS TO PRESBYTERIANS: FRENCH-CANADIAN IMMIGRANTS IN CENTRAL ILLINOIS. *American Presbyterians 1985 63(3): 285-298.*

Prints a narrative of the life of Charles Chiniquy, a French-Canadian priest who, in Canada during the 1830's-40's, preached total abstinence from alcohol, a position not popular among Catholics. Under pressure from his bishop, he ultimately left Canada and migrated to Illinois near Kankakee, in 1851. Soon afterward he and most of his congregation united with the Presbyterian Church.

CLARK, TOM

47. West, Ellis M. JUSTICE TOM CLARK AND AMERICAN CHURCH-STATE LAW. *J. of Presbyterian Hist. 1976 54(4): 387-404.*

Tom Clark (1899-) was an Associate Justice of the US Supreme Court, 1949-67. While on the Court he wrote major opinions in the areas of civil rights, separation of powers, antitrust, national security and church-state relations. His opinions in the cases of *US* v. *Seeger* and *Abington School District* v. *Schemp* were historic in church-state relations and of far reaching consequences. The latter struck down officially prescribed prayer and Bible-reading in the public schools. Points out that Clark, a very dedicated Presbyterian layman, was a constructive moderate who argued for the essential autonomy of religion and government but refused to support their complete separation.

COHEN, MORRIS RAPHAEL

48. Rosenfield, Leonora Cohen. THE JUDAIC VALUES OF A PHILOSOPHER: MORRIS RAPHAEL COHEN, 1880-1947. *Jewish Social Studies 1980 42(3-4): 189-214.*

The Jewish philosopher Morris Raphael Cohen espoused a number of Jewish values according to which he lived his life, including: 1) the welfare of world Jewry depends upon the liberalism of society, 2) every Jew should know something about his roots and Judaic heritage, 3) Jews must venerate learning and constantly probe for knowledge, 4) the Hebrew prophets must inspire Jews to spiritual values, universal truth, and eternity of ideas, 5) a Jew must be a loyal defender of his people, and 6) Jews must be actively committed to social justice, righteousness, and compassion. Cohen demonstrated many of these values through his work on behalf of the Conference on Jewish Relations, which he helped to found.

COLEMAN, BENJAMIN

49. Roeber, Anthony Gregg. "HER MERCHANDIZE . . . SHALL BE HOLINESS TO THE LORD": THE PROGRESS AND DECLINE OF PURITAN GENTILITY AT THE BRATTLE STREET CHURCH, BOSTON, 1715-1745. *New England Hist. and Geneal. Register 1977 131: 175-194.*

Examines the life and thought of Benjamin Coleman, pastor of Boston's Brattle Street Church and minister to many of the town's wealthy merchants. The congregation was at the center of a number of controversies which shook Massachusetts during 1715-40, most notably the great credit debates. Coleman's special mission was to bring the "gentility" of 18th-century England to Boston and blend it with Puritan piety. The Puritan gentility had a distinct social dimension. Coleman advocated a social hierarchy with the clergy at the top assisted by a mercantile elite serving as guardians of church and society. However, Coleman never adequately defined his concept of gentility. In the end his ideas were overwhelmed by changes in Puritan thought and in America's attitude toward the mother country.

COLLINS, MARY CLEMENTINE

50. Clow, Richmond L., ed. AUTOBIOGRAPHY OF MARY C. COLLINS, MISSIONARY TO THE WESTERN SIOUX. *South Dakota Historical Collections 1982 41: 1-66.*

Mary Clementine Collins describes her work as a missionary of the Congregational Church to the Western Sioux in South Dakota from 1875 to 1910. Collins discusses her religious upbringing, her assignment to the Oahe Mission, the condition of the Indians' lives near the mission, and her memories of friends and acquaintances, both white and Indian. Among the prominent figures she encountered were Sitting Bull and the many Indian agents assigned to the Sioux agencies in North and South Dakota. By 1900 Collins began to question government policies intended to lead to Indian self-sufficiency, and she aired her complaints in letters to the Indian commissioners and at the Lake Mohonk Conferences.

CONROY, GEORGE

51. Perin, Roberto. TROPPO ARDENTI SACERDOTI: THE CONROY MISSION REVISITED.
Can. Hist. Rev. (Canada) 1980 61(3): 283-304.

Reassesses the mission of George Conroy (1832-78), an Irish bishop and Apostolic Delegate to the province of Quebec in 1877-78. Worried about the French Canadian clergy's involvement in politics, the Holy See chose Cardinal Paul Cullen's protege to impose a solution elaborated in Rome. Conroy did not study the roots of the crisis within the Quebec Church, but rather sought to appease the ruling Liberal Party in Ottawa. In so doing, he transformed the Catholic Church from a vital institution, relatively free from the partisan manipulation characterizing Canadian life since the advent of responsible government in 1848, into a tool of the politicians. Until 1878, the Church had been a rampart against an aggressive Anglo-Saxon nationalism which sought to mold Canada in its image. After this date, it was much less effective in resisting the "political compromises" which led to the triumph of this nationalism.

COX, SAMUEL HANSON

52. Mounger, Dwyn Mecklin. SAMUEL HANSON COX: ANTI-CATHOLIC, ANTI-ANGLICAN, ANTI-CONGREGATIONAL ECUMENIST.
J. of Presbyterian Hist. 1977 55(4): 347-361.

Samuel Hanson Cox (1813-80) was a typical New School Presbyterian in his ecumenical aspirations: he worked energetically to promote interdenominational cooperation through numerous benevolence and mission societies to produce a wholly Protestant America. Thus his ecumenism was more limited than that of similar positions today, for it embraced only denominations which he regarded as "evangelical," which included only those practicing revivalism. He viewed Catholicism, Anglicanism, and the resurgent denominationalism of the 1840's as major threats to a triumphantly Protestant

America. To counterbalance such movements, he labored hard for the Evangelical Alliance and the American Alliance and to prevent a North-South schism in the New School Presbyterian Church. Yet all these efforts were doomed to fail because of the slavery issue. As Moderator of the New School in 1846 he was successful in preventing abolitionism from dividing the Church that year; yet division came 11 years later. In his zeal for ecumenism he had been prepared to sacrifice the slave upon the altar of evangelical unity.

CRAPSEY, ALGERNON SIDNEY

53. Swanton, Carolyn. DR. ALGERNON S. CRAPSEY: RELIGIOUS REFORMER.
Rochester Hist. 1980 42(1): 1-24.

Episcopal minister Algernon Sidney Crapsey (1847-1927) went to Rochester from New York City in 1879 to minister at St. Andrew's Church; focuses on his humanitarian work and concern for his parishioners, and his trial in an ecclesiastical court in 1906 for heresy; found guilty, he was forced to leave the church, but continued his work until his death.

CRAWFORD, ISABEL

54. Mondello, Salvatore. (ISABEL CRAWFORD AND THE KIOWAS).
ISABEL CRAWFORD: THE MAKING OF A MISSIONARY.
Foundations 1978 21(4): 322-339.

Presents the early life and education of Isabel Crawford, a missionary of the Women's American Baptist Home Missionary Society. Born in Canada in 1865, she became interested in the plight of the Indians through various family moves while a child. She received her training in Chicago, during which time she did considerable work in the slums. In June, 1893, she received word that she had been appointed to work as a missionary among the Kiowas of Elk Creek, Indian Territory.

ISABEL CRAWFORD AND THE KIOWA INDIANS.
Foundations 1979 22(1): 28-42.

Describes the labors of Isabel Crawford among the Kiowa
Indians in and near the Wichita Mountains of Oklahoma, 1893
to 1906. Her very successful work was abruptly terminated and
she was forced to leave the Indians because of her questionable
participation in a communion service.

ISABEL CRAWFORD, CHAMPION OF THE AMERICAN
INDIANS.
Foundations 1979 22(2): 99-115.

Discusses Isabel Crawford's life from 1907 to her death in 1961.

CUMINGS, JOHN

55. Emlen, Robert P. THE HARD CHOICES OF BROTHER
JOHN CUMINGS.
Hist. New Hampshire 1979 34(1): 54-65.

John Cumings (1829-1911) had joined the Shaker community at
Enfield, New Hampshire, with his family in 1844. His father and
brother left the Shakers in the 1860's. Although sorely tempted
to join them, John finally decided, in the 1870's, to stay with the
Shakers, who came to rely on his mechanical skills. He held the
Enfield community together until his death in 1911. In 1923 the
surviving Enfield Shakers moved to Canterbury.

CUTLER, TIMOTHY

56. Huber, Donald L. TIMOTHY CUTLER: THE
CONVERT AS CONTROVERSIALIST.
*Hist. Mag. of the Protestant Episcopal Church 1975 44(4):
489-496.*

In the autumn of 1722 Timothy Cutler, Rector at Yale,
converted to Anglicanism. From that time until 1730 he became
the chief protagonist of the Church of England in Massachusetts,
where the established church was the Congregational. He served
as rector of Christ Church, Boston. Delineates some of Cutler's
gadfly undertakings as he sought relief for the Anglican church
from the Congregationalists. In some instances he was
successful, in others he failed; but for the most part he was
successful in forcing important concessions from the
Congregationalists. For reasons unknown he gradually withdrew

from the arena, but only after he had made a mark for himself as controversialist.

D

DAVIES, DAVID JONES AND GWEN

57. Davies, Phillips G. DAVID JONES AND GWEN DAVIES, MISSIONARIES IN NEBRASKA TERRITORY, 1853-1860.
Nebraska Hist. 1979 60(1): 77-91.

David Jones Davies (1814-91) and his wife Gwen (1823-1910) were a missionary couple whose work among the Omaha Indians in eastern Nebraska spanned the years 1853-60. Both were born in Wales and furthered the work of the Calvinist Methodists in their missionary work.

DAWSON, WILLIAM

58. Hockman, Dan M. COMMISSARY WILLIAM DAWSON AND THE ANGLICAN CHURCH IN VIRGINIA, 1743-1752.
Historical Magazine of the Protestant Episcopal Church 1985 54(2): 125-149.

William Dawson served the last nine years of his life as commissary of the Anglican Church in Virginia. By wielding the combined power of his ecclesiastical office as commissary and his civil office as a member of the council, he did much to promote the welfare and interests of the Anglican Church in Virginia. As commissary, councillor, and as president of William and Mary College, Dawson emerged as an important and influential figure in colonial Virginia.

DEVOTION, EBENEZER

59. Noll, Mark A. EBENEZER DEVOTION: RELIGION AND SOCIETY IN REVOLUTIONARY CONNECTICUT.
Church Hist. 1976 45(3): 293-307.

Uses the career of Ebenezer Devotion as an example to explore the relationship between church and state in 18th-century New England. Because Devotion not only performed the normal range of ministerial functions but was involved in pre-Revolutionary politics, a study of his life reveals much about such interaction. Throughout his career, Devotion remained ultraconservative in ecclesiastical matters. He was among the opponents of the Great Awakening. In this controversy, he developed two opinions that would be important in his later political thinking. First, he came to view "covenant as an external, legal device through which external legal relationships were established." Second, Devotion defended his right as a minister to attend ecclesiastical councils not on the basis of scripture but because it was "a Liberty . . . that is given by the great Law of Nature." Both positions again manifested themselves in Devotion's opposition to the Stamp Act. His political life was part of and depended upon his religious ideology and ecclesiastical viewpoint.

DICKERSON, WILLIAM FISHER

60. Dickerson, Dennis C. WILLIAM FISHER DICKERSON: NORTHERN PREACHER/SOUTHERN PRELATE. *Methodist History 1985 23(3): 135-152.*

William Fisher Dickerson was one of the few formally educated pastors in the African Methodist Episcopal Church, the oldest black US denomination, and, prior to the Civil War, primarily a Northern institution. Still a young minister when his career was promoted by a series of important appointments, Dickerson was crowned with the pastorship of Sullivan Street Church in New York City at the age of 33 and was acclaimed for his sermons. He led a "Thinker's Course of Lectures" featuring leading black preachers and poets. At 36, Dickerson became the youngest bishop in his church. In 1881 he went to London to preach on the nature of Methodism to the Ecumenical Methodist Conference. While Dickerson's election ensured the continuation of Northern dominance in the church, he soon ran into revolt among Southern brethren who resisted that influence. He died in 1884, aged 41.

DOUGLASS, FREDERICK

61. Andrews, William L. FREDERICK DOUGLASS, PREACHER.
Am. Lit. 1982 54(4): 592-597.

Frederick Douglass began his speaking career in the North as a licensed preacher with the Zion Methodist Church in New Bedford, Massachusetts, during the 1840's. This professional preaching built on previous experience Douglass had as head of a black Sunday school in the South.

DOWIE, JOHN ALEXANDER

62. Heath, Alden R. APOSTLE IN ZION.
J. of the Illinois State Hist. Soc. 1977 70(2): 98-113.

John Alexander Dowie (1847-1907), Scottish evangelist and founder of the Divine Healing Association, came to the United States from Australia in 1888 and established in 1899 a new communitarian settlement based on strict prohibitions against alcohol, tobacco, labor unions, and doctors. His Christian Catholic Church's experiment at Zion, Illinois, drew thousands of converts, but his own megalomania caused followers to ultimately reject his leadership of that community.

DUBOSE, WILLIAM PORCHER

63. Luker, Ralph E. THE CRUCIBLE OF CIVIL WAR AND RECONSTRUCTION IN THE EXPERIENCE OF WILLIAM PORCHER DUBOSE.
South Carolina Hist. Mag. 1982 83(1): 50-71.

While William Porcher DuBose was better known abroad than at home, he was an American theologian whose experiences during the Civil War and Reconstruction periods shaped his thought. Born near Winnsboro in 1836 he attended Winnsboro Academy as a youth and at age 15 went to the Citadel, then to the University of Virginia, and finally to the Protestant Episcopal Church's Diocesan Seminary at Camden. There he met and studied with John H. Elliott. When the Civil War started, he joined the Holcombe Legion and despite several wounds saw action throughout the war. Drawing on the story of the prodigal son, he developed his thesis of "at-one-ment." He believed that "a Man's own self, when he has once truly come to himself, is his best and only experimental proof of God."

E

EDDY, MARY BAKER

64. Klein, Janice. ANN LEE AND MARY BAKER EDDY: THE PARENTING OF NEW RELIGIONS. *J. of Psychohistory 1979 6(3): 361-375.*

The Christian Science and Shaker religions, founded by Mary Baker Eddy and Ann Lee, respectively, had roots in the personal lives of their founders as well as in their social milieux. Focuses on the former, comparing the life experiences of Eddy and Lee, and suggests ways in which those experiences affected the theologies of the two religions.

65. Silberger, Julius, Jr. MARY BAKER EDDY. *Am. Heritage 1980 32(1): 56-64.*

Adapted from the author's recently published biography of Mary Baker Eddy (1821-1910), the founder and developer of Christian Science, who began her writing and founded the church in 1875 after a long and often unhappy earlier life. From the beginning, she sought to rid the church of any competitors to her own position. She founded the *Christian Science Monitor* in 1908, two years before her death.

EISENMANN, SYLVESTER

66. Wolff, Gerald W. FATHER SYLVESTER EISENMANN AND MARTY MISSION. *South Dakota Hist. 1975 5(4): 360-389.*

During 1918-48 Father Sylvester Eisenmann successfully ministered to Sioux Indians on the Yankton Reservation. He supported the Indians' welfare and was extremely generous in the time, effort, and money he invested in their behalf. A tireless worker, he was especially successful in raising funds and in constructing almost 30 major buildings at Marty. His accomplishments were offset somewhat by his paternalism and condescension. These attitudes grew out of his early years and training in southern Indiana. Thus his deep concern and great record of achievement for the Yankton Sioux were diminished because he treated his Indian charges as perpetual children. By rejecting their heritage and underestimating them as human beings, Father Sylvester did them a disservice.

ELIOT, JOHN

67. Sehr, Timothy J. JOHN ELIOT, MILLENNIALIST AND MISSIONARY.
Historian 1984 46(2): 187-203.

John Eliot was best known for his efforts in preaching the gospel to the Indians in early New England, and in producing the first Indian translation of the Bible. His work among the Indians was continually frustrated by politics in Massachusetts Bay Colony, particularly by King Philip's War in the mid 1670's and the revocation of the company charter in the mid 1680's. A millenarian, he believed for most of his life that he would live to see the millennium, a belief that he held until the 1680's, when he concluded that the millennium would occur sometime after his death.

ELLIS, EDWIN M.

68. Dosker, Nina Ellis. EDWIN M. ELLIS: MONTANA'S BICYCLING MINISTER.
Montana 1980 30(1): 42-51.

Edwin M. Ellis (1853-1940) was a Prebyterian minister and the Montana Superintendent of Sunday School Missions from 1884 until his retirement in 1927. As a minister, he served the Bitterroot Valley; his superintendent duties covered all Montana from his Helena headquarters. To facilitate his travel throughout rural Montana, Ellis used a Columbia Chainless Bicycle during 1892-1913. He became known as Montana's bicycling minister, and many of the churches and sunday schools he founded are still active today.

ELY, EDMUND F.

69. Hoover, Roy. "TO STAND ALONE IN THE WILDERNESS": EDMUND F. ELY, MISSIONARY. *Minnesota History 1985 49(7): 265-280.*

Presents the life and observations of Edmund F. Ely (1809-1882), who served as a lay missionary and teacher for the American Board of Commissioners for Foreign Missions among the Chippewa Indians in northern Minnesota and Wisconsin during 1833-49. His journals report much about his journey there and the first encounters with the land, the Indians, the work, and his competition and co-workers. While the years gave him more relaxed expectations about them all, he also acquired a large family and left his lonely occupation on the frontier.

ENGELHARDT, ZEPHYRIN

70. Burrus, Ernest J. A DEDICATION TO THE MEMORY OF ZEPHYRIN ENGELHARDT, O.F.M., 1851-1934. *Arizona and the West 1976 18(3): 212-216.*

German-born emigrant Charles Engelhardt (1851-1934) changed his Christian name to Zephyrin when he entered a seminary. After schooling and ordination, he had numerous assignments throughout the country in Indian missions and editorial work. In 1901 he was sent to Mission Santa Barbara in California, where he remained until his death. He was a prodigious collector of documents, manuscripts, and rare editions of Southwestern and Western history. He published "an astounding number" of "ponderous tomes" and articles on missionary activity in the Spanish Borderlands of the Southwest.

F

FIELD, ELIZA AND PETER

71. Smith, Donald B. THE TRANSATLANTIC COURTSHIP OF THE REVEREND PETER JONES. *Beaver (Canada) 1977 308(1): 4-13.*

Peter Jones, part Ojibwa, became a Methodist preacher in the 1820's and was successful in converting many of the Indians around Lake Ontario. In 1831 he was sent to England to solicit funds for the missions. He made more than 150 appearances, was successful, and met Eliza Field, daughter of a wealthy factory owner near London. She became interested in mission work, and in him. Jones proposed marriage, which she accepted, though her father resisted for some time. After consent was given, her father found out that Jones' father was still alive, and had two wives. Yet, in 1833, in New York, the couple was married.

FIELDE, ADELE M.

72. Hoyt, Frederick B. "WHEN A FIELD WAS FOUND TOO DIFFICULT FOR A MAN, A WOMAN SHOULD BE SENT": ADELE M. FIELDE IN ASIA, 1865-1890. *Historian 1982 44(3): 314-334.*

Adele M. Fielde, a transitional figure, illustrates the changing emphasis of the Protestant mission movement from wives to single women as evangelists. Recounts Fielde's life, including her introduction to the Orient in 1865, her missionary work as an American Baptist in Siam, her assignment to Swatow in China in 1872, and her permanent return to the United States in 1890. The major focus of her life as both a missionary and reformer was the condition of women and the reformation of society.

FOX, PAUL

73. Benkart, Paula. PAUL FOX, PRESBYTERIAN MISSION AND POLISH AMERICANS. *J. of Presbyterian Hist. 1982 60(4): 301-313.*

Although he set out to convert the staunchly Catholic Polish Americans to Protestantism, the Polish-born Paul Fox (b. 1875) eventually had to scale down his aspirations and be content simply to acquaint the Poles with Protestant beliefs, a process he felt was no threat to their ethnicity. Yet the course his own career took, the ties he developed with English-speaking Americans, and the social and psychological distance that began to grow between Fox and other Polish immigrants all illustrate his acceptance of how predominant American values could and did draw an individual apart from his own ethnic group. Emphasizes Fox's Presbyterian ministry among Polish immigrants in Baltimore and Chicago.

FRIEDMAN, WILLIAM STERNE

74. Hornbein, Marjorie. DENVER'S RABBI WILLIAM S. FRIEDMAN: HIS IDEAS AND INFLUENCE. *Western States Jewish Hist. Q. 1981 13(2): 142-154.*

Rabbi William Sterne Friedman (1868-1944), a conservative and an outspoken anti-Zionist, was sometimes accused of denying the ethnicity of Jews and of promoting their assimilation. On the contrary, he believed in a strong Jewish identity and adherenceto Judaism. At the same time he preached the duty of patriotism for the American Jew, who should be an American first.

FURNESS, WILLIAM HENRY

75. Hoffmann, R. Joseph. WILLIAM HENRY FURNESS: THE TRANSCENDENTALIST DEFENSE OF THE GOSPELS. *New England Q. 1983 56(2): 238-260.*

William Henry Furness, pastor of the First Congregational Unitarian Church of Philadelphia, published in 1836 *Remarks on the Four Gospels,* in which he tried to demonstrate his long-held belief that Christianity was the religion of nature. Examining Furness's thinking and writings in juxtaposition with mainline Boston Unitarians and Harvard scholars such as Andrews Norton indicates his divergence from their theology, especially in the interpretation of miracles. Furness saw no authentic revelation of religious truth that depended for verification on operations outside the natural order or beyond the scope of human reason. He was the most consistent advocate of a transcendentalist remedy to the dissolvent tendencies of German biblical scholarship.

G

GALLAND, ISAAC

76. Cook, Lyndon W. ISAAC GALLAND: MORMON BENEFACTOR.
Brigham Young U. Studies 1979 19(3): 261-284.

Isaac Galland (1791-1858) settled in Iowa and speculated in the Half-Breed Tract in Lee County. He interceded with the territorial government to insure a favorable reception of the Mormons and, in 1839, sold them land and converted to their faith. Joseph Smith instructed him to handle some of the Mormons' land transactions. For unknown reasons, he stopped his land activities for the Mormons and left the faith in the 1840's, but continued to associate with them until his death.

GALLITZIN, DEMETRIUS

77. Kring, Hilda Adam. PRINCE GALLITZIN, THE SAINT OF THE ALLEGHENIES.
Keystone Folklore 1984 3(1): 11-17.

Russian Prince Demetrius Gallitzin (alias Father Augustine Smith) was legendary for his help to the needy of western Pennsylvania as the first Catholic priest ordained in the United States. Gallitzin's memory lives in a Halloween ritual at St. Francis College in Loretto, Pennsylvania.

GEFFEN, TOBIAS

78. Kaganoff, Nathan M. AN ORTHODOX RABBINATE IN THE SOUTH: TOBIAS GEFFEN, 1870-1970.
Am. Jewish Hist. 1983 73(1): 56-70.

Tobias Geffen left his Lithuanian homeland after the 1903 Kishinev pogrom, served briefly as a rabbi in New York City and Canton, Ohio, and then for nearly 60 years was rabbi of the Congregation Shearith Israel of Atlanta, where, in addition to supporting community educational and charity enterprises, he established religious schools, helped make local food products kosher, served the needs of Jewish soldiers and prisoners, and deftly handled so many religious issues that for years he was recognized as the Orthodox authority for Southern Jews. Though not as unemotional as the typical Lithuanian rabbinic scholar, he epitomized the immigrant rabbi, whose Old World Orthodoxy could not survive into the second generation.

GEIGER, MAYNARD J.

79. Nunis, Doyce B., Jr. IN MEMORIAM: FATHER MAYNARD J. GEIGER, O.F.M.
California Hist. Q. 1977 56(3): 275-276.

Eulogizes Father Maynard J. Geiger (1901-1977), Franciscan father, archivist of Mission Santa Barbara for almost 40 years, and historian of Franciscan missionary activity in North America, particularly Hispanic California. His published writings included 13 books, among them *The Life and Times of Fray Junipero Serra, Mission Santa Barbara, 1782-1965,* and *Franciscan Missionaries in Hispanic California, 1769-1848.* In addition, he wrote almost 200 articles and for 15 years was editor of *Provincial Annals.* As a speaker he was much in demand by historical groups, and his correspondence with teachers and students was international in scale.

80. Nunis, Doyce B., Jr. A DEDICATION TO THE MEMORY OF MAYNARD J. GEIGER, O.F.M., 1901-1977.
Arizona and the West 1978 20(3): 198-202.

Franciscan Fr. Maynard Joseph Geiger (1901-77) completed his philosophical and theological studies in California and was ordained to the priesthood. His M.A. work at St. Bonaventure College, New York, in English and Spanish were preparatory for his doctorate in Hispanic American history in 1937 at The Catholic University of America, Washington, D. C. His professional career was spent as archivist and historian at Mission Santa Barbara, California. His early writings focused on Spanish Florida. Later his scholarship was concerned with the Franciscan missionaries in California, particularly Junipero Serra.

GOLDSTEIN, DAVID

81. Campbell, Debra. A CATHOLIC SALVATION ARMY:
DAVID GOLDSTEIN, PIONEER LAY EVANGELIST.
Church Hist. 1983 52(3): 322-332.

David Goldstein, a convert from Judaism and socialism, became
a lay Catholic street lecturer. Goldstein, with the help of Martha
Moore Avery, founded the Catholic Truth Guild in 1917. During
the following quarter-century, Goldstein and his associates used
methods like those employed by evangelists like Billy Sunday,
traveling across the country to increase Catholic Church
membership.

GRANT, RACHEL RIDGWAY IVINS

82. Walker, Ronald W. RACHEL R. GRANT: THE
CONTINUING LEGACY OF THE FEMININE IDEAL.
Dialogue 1982 15(3): 105-121.

Rachel Ridgway Ivins Grant was born in New Jersey. She
converted to Mormonism at an early age, living at first in
Nauvoo, Illinois, and later in Utah. In 1855, at the age of 32, she
married Jedediah Morgan Grant. Their son, Herbert, eventually
became president of the Mormon Church. Her husband died in
1856, after which she and her son lived a life of poverty and
hardship until she started a boardinghouse. She also became
president of the local branch of the Mormon Relief Society,
retiring at the age of 82. Throughout her life she was known for
her firm moral strength.

GREEN, JACOB

83. Noll, Mark A. OBSERVATIONS ON THE
RECONCILIATION OF POLITICS AND RELIGION IN
REVOLUTIONARY NEW JERSEY: THE CASE OF JACOB
GREEN.
J. of Presbyterian Hist. 1976 54(2): 217-237.

Jacob Green's perception of the distinction between the church
and the world is the key to understanding the nature of his
participation in Revolutionary events. The thinking which
distinguished church and world in his ecclesiology enabled him

to upbraid colonial society for religious and moral shortcomings. He took the Whig view of the Revolutionary crisis seriously; at the same time he was able to transcend libertarian categories and to call American society to account by a higher law to which he owed first allegience. Green's case militates against Bernard Bailyn's conclusion concerning the source of moral reform in Revolutionary America. Green's criticism of society proceeded not primarily from a libertarian perspective but from a religious orientation derived from Edwardsean theology.

84. Noll, Mark A.   JACOB GREEN'S PROPOSAL FOR SEMINARIES.
J. of Presbyterian Hist. 1980 58(3): 210-222.

The first Presbyterian seminary in America was not established until 1812. However, the Reverend Jacob Green (1722-90) thought of such a school. Education was of the utmost importance to him, both in the pastorate as well as in his concern for a better-trained ministry. At that time young men studying for the ministry after completing college studied under an "approved divine." On 22 November 1775 he sent a letter to his Congregational friend, the Reverend Joseph Bellamy, in which he laid out his plan for a theological seminary. The letter arose out of his concern about the shortage of ministers and his conviction that the current effort to train them was not succeeding. Reprints the previously unpublished letter.

H

HARTSFIELD, GREEN W.

85. Poe, William A.   NORTH LOUISIANA SOCIAL LIFE AS REFLECTED IN THE MINISTRY OF GREEN W. HARTSFIELD, 1860-96.
North Louisiana Hist. Assoc. J. 1981 12(1): 1-11.

Green W. Hartsfield (b. 1833) entered the Baptist ministry at the age of 26. Known as "the peoples' pastor" during his three decades of ministry, he served numerous churches in northern Louisiana. His ministry to blacks and whites, his aversion to revelry, and his and the area's concern with high infant mortality, are all reflected in the article.

86. Poe, William A. THE STORY OF A FRIENDSHIP AND A BOOK: W. E. PAXTON AND GREEN W. HARTSFIELD. *Louisana Hist. 1981 22(2): 167-182.*

Discusses the friendship between Baptist ministers W. E. Paxton and Green W. Hartsfield. Paxton was instrumental in the formation of the Baptist Historical Society in 1860. He gathered data from all over Louisiana and by 1881 had completed a manuscript of some 500 pages, which was destined to become one of the most treasured books in Louisiana history. It was entitled *History of the Baptists of Louisiana from the Earliest Times to the Present.* Because of his untimely death in 1883, the book only saw print because of Hartsfield's attention to the project.

HARTZELL, JOSEPH C.

87. Loveland, Anne C. THE "SOUTHERN WORK" OF THE REVEREND JOSEPH C. HARTZELL, PASTOR OF AMES CHURCH IN NEW ORLEANS, 1870-1873. *Louisiana Hist. 1975 16(4): 391-407.*

"Like most other Northern Methodist missionaries to the South, Hartzell saw no conflict in linking religious endeavors and Republican politics." Hartzell supervised three Methodist institutions for Negroes: Union Normal School, Thomson Institute, and the Freedmen's Orphan Home which combined educational and missionary efforts. The response of Southern Whites to the educational and missionary work of the Northern Methodists among the freedmen was generally unsympathetic. Another reason for the loss of support was the Republicans ultimately abandoned the social and political goals of Reconstruction.

HELLER, MAXIMILIAN

88. Zola, Gary P. REFORM JUDAISM'S PIONEER ZIONIST: MAXIMILIAN HELLER. *Am. Jewish Hist. 1984 73(4): 375-397.*

Czech Maximilian Heller, disciple of Reform leader Isaac M. Wise, struggled long and against great opposition to merge Zionism with Reform Judaism. More than the handful of other

Reform Zionists, Heller not only developed an integrated philosophy of the two movements but also brought Zionism into the institutional structures of Reform Judaism, particularly Hebrew Union College and the Central Conference of American Rabbis, of which he became president in 1910. By the time of his death in 1929, Zionism had a respectable, albeit still small, place in Reform Judaism.

HENRY, HENRY ABRAHAM

89. Henry, Marcus H. HENRY ABRAHAM HENRY: SAN FRANCISCO RABBI, 1857-1869.
Western States Jewish Hist. Q. 1977 10(1): 31-37.

Henry Abraham Henry (1806-79) came to the United States from England in 1849. He served congregations in Ohio and New York before coming to San Francisco in 1857. He was minister of San Francisco's Sherith Israel (Polish) synagogue, from 1857-69. A popular lecturer, he officiated at the consecration of many synagogues and the dedications of secular institutions. Rabbi Henry contributed many articles to American Jewish journals. He published his two-part *Synopsis of Jewish History* in 1859. In 1860 he started and edited the weekly *Pacific Messenger*. In 1864 he issued his volume of *Discourses on the Book of Genesis*. His religious views were conservative. He upheld the dignity of his profession to the admiration of both Jews and Christians.

HERBERG, WILL

90. Siegel, Seymour. WILL HERBERG, 1955.
Modern Age 1982 26(3-4): 276-279.

Pays tribute to Will Herberg. Born in Russia, he came to the United States at an early age. In his youth an ardent Communist, he soon became disillusioned and returned to his Jewish roots after hearing a lecture by Reinhold Niebuhr. He studied at Jewish Theological Seminary and taught social philosophy and Judaic thought at Drew University in Madison, New Jersey, until his retirement in 1976. His *Catholic-Protestant-Jew* (1955) was an influential work in American religious sociology. Politically conservative, he was religion editor for William Buckley's *National Review* and editorial advisor to *Modern Age*.

HERSHMAN, ABRAHAM MOSES

91. Hershman, Ruth and Hershman, Eiga. RABBI
ABRAHAM M. HERSHMAN.
Michigan Jewish Hist. 1981 21(2): 16-31.

Traces the life of Rabbi Abraham Moses Hershman (1880-1959)
from his roots in Lithuania, where he received a traditional
Jewish education as a boy, to his later work as a rabbi in Detroit
after his ordination in 1906, and his efforts for Zionism; and
discusses the scholarly endeavors which Hershman undertook
after his retirement in 1946, especially his translation of a
portion of the *Code of Maimonides.*

92. Anderson, Grant K. SAMUEL D. HINMAN AND THE
OPENING OF THE BLACK HILLS.
Nebraska Hist. 1979 60(4): 520-542.

Episcopal missionary Samuel D. Hinman acted also as an
explorer, treaty maker, and interpreter during negotiations for
the Black Hills. As a missionary he devoted three decades to
converting the Sioux Indians to Christianity and revising their
way of life. During the critical years, 1874-76, he took part in all
governmental dealings with the Sioux.

HONCHARENKO, AHAPI

93. Buryk, Michael. AGAPIUS HONCHARENKO:
PORTRAIT OF A UKRAINIAN AMERICAN KOZAK.
Ukrainian Q. 1976 32(1): 16-36.

Agapius Honcharenko (1832-1916) was the first Ukrainian
priest in the United States. Threatened and pursued by Russian
authorities for his anti-tsarist writings in radical periodicals
published abroad, Honcharenko emigrated to the United States
in 1865. The first issue of his newspaper *The Alaska Herald* in
1868 marked the realization of his dream of establishing a
Russian publishing house in America. However, Honcharenko's
attacks on the monopolistic practices of American companies in
Alaska and his criticism of anti-Chinese feeling in the West
provoked slander and physical threats which forced his
resignation as editor in 1872. Following this Honcharenko
hoped to found a cooperative Ukrainian community in

California, but this plan also failed. His remaining life was spent on his farm "Ukraina."

HOPKINS, JOHN HENRY

94. Mullin, Robert Bruce. RITUALISM, ANTI-ROMANISM, AND THE LAW IN JOHN HENRY HOPKINS. *Hist. Mag. of the Protestant Episcopal Church 1981 50(4): 377-390.*

John Henry Hopkins was Episcopal bishop of Vermont during 1832-68. During his episcopacy, he participated in numerous controversies that arose in the Episcopal Church. Among the major ones this study centers on are his views on ritualism and Roman Catholicism. He attempted to anchor the teaching of the church upon the unchangeable law of divine truth as found in Scripture and tradition. By so doing he hoped to be free to examine these and other questions facing the church. He employed this methodology to question Roman Catholic teachings and to defend ritualistic practices. What seemed contradictory to others was consistency to him. He had few disciples, and he left no successors in his peculiar emphasis on law and doctrine. Nevertheless he made a significant impact upon the 19th-century Episcopal Church.

HOPKINS, SAMUEL

95. Conforti, Joseph. SAMUEL HOPKINS AND THE REVOLUTIONARY ANTISLAVERY MOVEMENT. *Rhode Island Hist. 1979 38(2): 39-49.*

A Congregational minister in Newport, Rhode Island, Samuel Hopkins, began speaking out against slavery and the slave trade in the 1770's and went on to become a leading figure in the New England antislavery movement until his death in 1803.

HORNER, RALPH CECIL

96. Ross, Brian R. RALPH CECIL HORNER: A METHODIST SECTARIAN DEPOSED. *J. of the Can. Church Hist. Soc. (Canada) 1977 19(1-2):94-103.*

Finding salvation through an evangelical experience in 1872, Ralph C. Horner dedicated himself to winning souls through evangelism and was ordained a minister in the Montreal Conference of the Methodist Church of Canada in 1887. Horner was very successful as an evangelist but found considerable problems with the authorities of the church. They found his methods excessive and discovered that he would not follow their orders. Though told to accept an assignment as a regular minister, Horner refused to do so. The Conference leaders tried to work out an arrangement with him but to no avail. In 1894 Horner was deposed from the ministry of the Methodist Church. Ultimately, in 1900, he organized his own successful Holiness Movement Church in Canada. His strong belief in freedom and his self-confidence in the rightness of his mission made him unable to accept direction from others.

HUNTER, JAMES

97. Peake, F. A. THE ACHIEVEMENTS AND FRUSTRATIONS OF JAMES HUNTER. *J. of the Can. Church Hist. Soc. (Canada) 1977 19(3-4): 138-165.*

Describes the missionary work of the Anglican priest James Hunter, an Englishman, in what is now western Canada, during 1844-64. Hunter maintained good relations with the Hudson's Bay Company which had power in the area and made significant contributions to the missionary effort. First, he translated the *Book of Common Prayer* and other religious works into the Cree Indian language. Second, he worked hard to expand Anglican missionary efforts throughout the area known as Rupert's Land, despite some opposition from the Company. His attempts in this area were rewarded by success, but in 1864 Hunter decided to return to England permanently. Ostensibly he did so for the education of his children, but he also may have been frustrated in his desire to occupy a position of leadership within the Church. Upon his return to England, his opportunities in this area were greatly improved.

HUTCHINSON, ANNE

98. Maclear, J. F. ANNE HUTCHINSON AND THE MORTALIST HERESY.
New England Q. 1981 54(1): 74-103.

Modern historians of the Antinomian controversy and Anne Hutchinson's 1638 ecclesiastical trial in Massachusetts Bay have ignored Anne's mortalism. The "Soul Sleepers" or mortalists, including Hutchinson, rejected the belief in the conscious immortality of the soul and instead asserted that bodies and souls perish together at death. Hutchinson's belief was both part of the historic Reformation and harbinger of that religious experimentation that characterized many interregnum Puritans. The episode was significant in Puritan history. It shows that the disappearance of mortalism was not quite as total as John Winthrop asserted, clarifies Hutchinson's personality and the nature of her threat to the infant colony, and makes her skepticism about the soul's immortality comprehensible within the context of Continental sectarianism, Stuart Puritanism, and 17th-century intellectual history.

I

ILLOWY, BERNARD

99. Ellenson, David. A JEWISH LEGAL DECISION BY RABBI BERNARD ILLOWY OF NEW ORLEANS AND ITS DISCUSSION IN NINETEENTH CENTURY EUROPE.
Am. Jewish Hist. 1979 69(2): 174-195.

Dr. Bernard Illowy (1812-71) immigrated to the United States in 1853 and became one of the first Orthodox rabbis in the country. He engaged in disputes with Reform rabbis and rendered decisions in matters of Jewish canon law. In 1864, he placed a ban on a mohel who circumcised sons born to Jewish fathers and non-Jewish mothers. His decision was upheld by various European Orthodox rabbis, including Esriel Hildesheimer, but was contested by Rabbi Zvi Hirsch Kalischer. The episode demonstrates the lax state of Orthodoxy in mid-19th-century America, and shows that Illowy was respected by his European rabbinical colleagues.

INGLIS, JOHN

100. Mount, Graeme S. and Mount, Joan E. BISHOP JOHN
INGLIS AND HIS ATTITUDE TOWARD RACE IN
BERMUDA IN THE ERA OF EMANCIPATION.
J. of the Can. Church Hist. Soc. (Canada) 1983 25(1): 25-32.

The Right Reverend John Inglis, Anglican bishop of Nova
Scotia, espoused a liberal racial policy in Bermuda between
1825 and 1839. In the strict racial segregation of Bermuda,
Inglis promoted black education and black membership in the
Anglican Church. Before emancipation in 1832, Inglis insisted
that black slaves attend divine services with their white masters.
Bermudian blacks later left the Anglican Church in droves
because of the racist episcopacy of Inglis's successor, Bishop
Edward Feild.

IRELAND, ELLEN

101. Johnston, Patricia Condon. REFLECTED GLORY: THE
STORY OF ELLEN IRELAND.
Minnesota Hist. 1982 48(1): 13-23.

Ellen Ireland, sister of John, the first archbishop of St. Paul,
spent 72 years as Sister Seraphine, an educator, administrator,
and, for 39 years, mother superior of the Sisters of St. Joseph of
Corondelet's St. Paul Province (Minnesota and the Dakotas).
Her influence was felt by 30 schools, five hospitals, and the
College of St. Catherine.

J

JACKSON, SHELDON

102. Hinckley, Ted C. SHELDON JACKSON: GILDED
AGE APOSTLE.
Journal of the West 1984 23(1): 16-25.

Profiles Sheldon Jackson, an American Protestant missionary
who helped organize 23 churches before he left his first post in
Minnesota for the Far West. Once there, his promotional skills

were polished and his work earned him the title "Presbyterian Superintendent of the Rockies." He also worked extensively in Alaska establishing mission schools, one of which, the Sheldon Jackson College of Sitka, survives today.

JANSON, KRISTOFER

103. Draxten, Nina. KRISTOFER JANSON'S BEGINNING MINISTRY.
Norwegian-American Studies 1967 23: 126-174.

Kristofer Janson came to America in October 1881, at the urging of Rasmus B. Anderson, initially in order to make a lecture tour of the Midwest in the hopes of stirring interest in a liberal religious organization for Norwegian Americans. Upon his arrival, he was accepted into the ministry in the Unitarian Church and from there moved to Minneapolis, Minnesota, where he began setting up his ministry and recruiting members for his congregation. Though he first met with solid criticism as a freethinker, he eventually gained popular acceptance and was able to establish himself among the Scandinavians in the community. In March 1882, he returned to his native Norway to fetch his wife and family in order to establish a permanent home in the United States.

JASTROW, MORRIS

104. Wechsler, Harold S. PULPIT OR PROFESSORIATE: THE CASE OF MORRIS JASTROW.
American Jewish History 1985 74(4): 338-355.

Morris Jastrow, after training for the rabbinate in Europe during 1881-85, rejected the post held by his father at Rodef Shalom in Philadelphia, and instead chose an academic career in Semitics at the University of Pennsylvania, not because of a loss of religious conviction or commitment due to his exposure to modern philological studies in Europe, but because, upon return, he became pessimistic about his ability to alter significantly the course of American Jewish belief and practice set by Isaac Mayer Wise and his Hebrew Union College.

JOHNSON, SAMUEL (1822-82)

105. Mueller, Roger C. SAMUEL JOHNSON, AMERICAN TRANSCENDENTALIST: A SHORT BIOGRAPHY. *Essex Inst. Hist. Collections 1979 115(1): 9-67.*

Johnson was born in Salem, Massachusetts, in 1822. He graduated from Harvard in 1842 and from Harvard Divinity School in 1846. Before leaving Divinity School he collaborated with a classmate, Samuel Longfellow, on *A Book of Hymns for Public and Private Devotion* (Boston, 1846) in which they tried to make hymns "more acceptable to Unitarians in general." Initially a "conservative Unitarian," Johnson, spurred by Theodore Parker's influence, developed his own ministerial model which would go beyond Parker's Christianity into Universal Religion. After graduation Johnson became involved with abolitionist activities which resulted in a speaking engagement to the Lynn congregation and to the formation in 1853 of the Lynn Free Church and Johnson as its minister. For the next 17 years Johnson used the Lynn ministry to establish the outlines of his ideal religion grounded in Transcendentalism. Johnson became increasingly interested in Asian religions and resigned in 1870 to devote more time to his manuscripts on Oriental religions. Until his death in North Andover in 1882 Johnson wrote his *Oriental Religions and Their Relation to Universal Religion* series on India, China, and Persia. "Neither the facts nor the methods of his Oriental books are of much value today," but Johnson significantly affected the "development of Transcendentalism as a religious, philosophical, literary, and educational movement."

JONES, DAVID THOMAS

106. Bredin, Thomas F. THE REVEREND DAVID JONES: MISSIONARY AT RED RIVER 1823-38. *Beaver (Canada) 1981 312(2): 47-52.*

The diary of David Thomas Jones (1798-1844), evangelist, teacher, and Anglican chaplain to the Hudson's Bay Company, records his life at the Red River Settlement during 1823-38. He arrived at age 25 at York Factory. His firm yet effective dealings with the Indians brought him considerable success. The rigors of his first winter were to be the worst he ever experienced. His pleas to the Church Missionary Society for a co-worker were answered in 1825 when William Cockran was sent out just in time to witness "(t)he greatest natural disaster," the flood of 1825-26. Two years later Jones traveled to England, married, and returned to the settlement.

JONES, JAMES PARNELL

107. Curtis, Peter H. A QUAKER AND THE CIVIL WAR: THE LIFE OF JAMES PARNELL JONES. *Quaker Hist. 1978 67(1): 35-41.*

Raised as a Quaker in Maine, James Parnell Jones spent two years at Haverford College, and developed a passion for antislavery and temperance reforms in reaction to the "hypocrisy" of conservative, Philadelphia Quakers. He taught school, and graduated from the University of Michigan in 1856, shifting toward the reformist tenets of Progressive or Congregational Friends in the area. When he returned to Maine in 1861 and joined its 7th Regiment, he was disowned, but felt himself still a Friend in all respects except in fighting the war for freedom and union.

JONES, RUFUS

108. Alten, Diana. RUFUS JONES AND THE AMERICAN FRIEND: A QUEST FOR UNITY. *Quaker History 1985 74(1): 41-48.*

Rufus Jones edited the Philadelphia *Friends Review,* which merged with the Chicago *Christian Worker* to form the Philadelphia *American Friend,* for 20 years, while teaching philosophy at Haverford College. His charismatic speaking and writing probably prevented a schism between evangelical and modernist Quakers.

K

KAPLAN, MORDECAI M.

109. Scult, Melvin. MORDECAI M. KAPLAN: CHALLENGES AND CONFLICTS IN THE TWENTIES. *Am. Jewish Hist. Q. 1977 61(3): 401-416.*

Mordecai M. Kaplan was an immigrant who grew up on the lower East Side of New York City and who tried to reconcile his Orthodox Jewish upbringing with the new American culture. The struggle assumed both intellectual and spiritual aspects and was the basis for Kaplan's ambivalence toward the Jewish Theological Seminary where he served as head of its Teacher's Institute and as professor of Homiletics. Analyzes the gradual development of reconstructionist thoughts, clashes with Orthodoxy and seminary colleagues, relations with administrators and the lengthy negotiations with Stephen Wise and the Jewish Institute of Religion.

KERR, WILLIAM JASPER

110. McIlvenna, Don E. and Wax, Darold D. W. J. KERR, LAND-GRANT PRESIDENT IN UTAH AND OREGON, 1900-1908. *Oregon Historical Quarterly 1984 85(4): 387-405.*

William Jasper Kerr joined the faculty of Brigham Young College, Logan, Utah, in 1887 and became president in 1894. In 1900 he was appointed president of the Agricultural College of Utah, Logan. His efforts to upgrade the college and broaden course offerings brought charges of wasteful competition with the University of Utah. Political differences with Governor John C. Cutler and charges of Mormon Church dictation of college affairs contributed to Kerr's resignation in 1907. Consolidation of the college and university was a major issue during his tenure, but the necessary constitutional amendment failed in the legislature.

KIMBALL, HEBER C.

111. Kimball, Stanley B. BRIGHAM AND HEBER. *Brigham Young U. Studies 1978 18(3): 396-409.*

Heber C. Kimball's friendship with Brigham Young began in 1829 when both were 27-year-old artisans in Monroe County, New York. Following similar paths into Mormonism, the two men shared many common experiences in the faith as missionaries, as leaders in Nauvoo and during the exodus westward, and as ecclesiastics in the Utah community. Details their parallel careers as Young assumed the church presidency and Kimball became his first counselor. Near the end of his life, Kimball began to experience self-doubts about his and Young's contributions to Mormonism. Despite outside criticisms and his own fears and suppositions, Kimball remained loyal to Young. Kimball died on 22 June 1868.

KIMBALL, SPENCER W.

112. Kimball, Edward L. "I SUSTAIN HIM AS A PROPHET, I LOVE HIM AS AN AFFECTIONATE FATHER." *Dialogue 1978 11(4): 48-62.*

Transcript of an October 1978 interview between *Dialogue* and Edward L. Kimball, the youngest son of Spencer W. Kimball, President of the Church of Jesus Christ of the Latter Day Saints. Kimball, with his brother Andrew, wrote a biography of their father, published in 1977, based on interviews with their parents, friends of the family and leaders of the church, journal entries, personal letters, and family anecdotes. The process of writing the biography made it possible to check the growth of myths about the leader of the Mormon church. Kimball shares his special pride in his father's revelation allowing blacks to hold the priesthood in the Mormon church.

KING, MARTIN LUTHER, JR.

113. Oates, Stephen B. THE INTELLECTUAL ODYSSEY OF MARTIN LUTHER KING. *Massachusetts Rev. 1981 22(2): 301-320.*

Gives biography of Martin Luther King, Jr. (1929-68), American Negro clergyman, civil rights leader, and author, from kindergarten to his doctoral graduation in 1955 from Boston University. While a student at Morehouse College, he decided to enter the ministry. Mentions the faculty members who influenced this decision. He next attended Crozer Seminary. Describes the influences felt there, especially the writings of Walter Rauschenbusch. He enrolled in the doctoral program in systematic theology at Boston University, where he came under the influence of Edgar Sheffield Brightman and his disciple, Lotan Harold DeWolf. Here he tried to reconcile the conflict between relativism and idealism. In so doing he read widely in Sigmund Freud, and accepted his theories in part. On graduation King accepted a pastorate in Montgomery, Alabama.

KLAWITER, ANTHONY

114. Cuba, Stanley L. REV. ANTHONY KLAWITER: POLISH ROMAN AND NATIONAL CATHOLIC BUILDER-PRIEST.
Polish Am. Studies 1983 40(2): 59-92.

Father Anthony Klawiter was an unusual priest whose wanderings, assignments, and changes in church affiliation earned him such titles as "circuit rider," "transcontinental priest," and the "fallen-away priest." Father Klawiter held church assignments from the state of Washington to Massachusetts and from New Jersey to Manitoba, Canada. A priest filled with missionary zeal and Polish nationalism, Father Klawiter's controversial career reflects the internecine wars waged in Polish-American communities during the 19th and early 20th centuries.

KRAUSKOPF, JOSEPH

115. Sutherland, John F. RABBI JOSEPH KRAUSKOPF OF PHILADELPHIA: THE URBAN REFORMER RETURNS TO THE LAND.
Am. Jewish Hist. Q. 1978 67(4): 342-362.

Joseph Krauskopf (1858-1923) came to the United States as a 14-year-old. He graduated with the first class of four at Hebrew Union College in 1883 and was Philadelphia's foremost reform rabbi during 1887-1922. He introduced English into both services and the religious school, popularized the Jewish Sundry Services, and drafted the Pittsburgh Platform of 1885. His great concern with social reform led him into close cooperation with Jacob Riis. After a visit with Leo Tolstoy at Yasnaya Polyana, Krauskopf became the driving spirit of the Jewish "back-to-the land" movement and of the National Farm School, today known as the Delaware Valley College of Science and Agriculture, the only private agricultural school in the country. Thoroughly part of America's urban milieu, Krauskopf nevertheless sought to modify it with the agrarian myth, an urban-agrarian ambivalence which still influences American thought and action.

L

LANKERSHIM, ISAAC

116. Kramer, William M. and Stern, Norton B. ISAAC LANKERSHIM OF THE SAN FERNANDO VALLEY: JEWISH-BORN BAPTIST.
Southern California Quarterly 1985 67(1): 25-33.

Born in Bavaria, Isaac Lankershim came to the United States in 1836 and settled in St. Louis. In 1842, he married Annis Moore and converted from Judaism to the Baptist faith, though retaining his Jewish family ties. Attracted to California during the gold rush era, Lankershim became a successful wheat grower and sheep raiser. In 1869, he and other investors purchased 60,000 acres in the San Fernando Valley, forming the San Fernando Sheep Company and later the Los Angeles Farming and Milling Company. At his death in 1882, Lankershim was eulogized for his pioneering efforts in promoting agricultural development and his reputation for integrity in business.

LARSON, LARS

117. Canuteson, Richard L. LARS AND MARTHA LARSON: "WE DO WHAT WE CAN FOR THEM."
Norwegian-American Studies 1972 25: 142-166.

In 1807, as part of a commercial venture on board a ship bound to sell lumber, Lars Larson was seized by the British (with whom Norway-Denmark was at war) and imprisoned for seven years. During this time he converted to Quakerism and upon his 1814 return to Norway began teaching the tenets of that religion for which he was severely punished by the Norwegian government. In 1825, after continual denial of their religious freedom, a group of Norwegians immigrated to the United States. Most settled in Kendall Colony, New York, but Larson and his family moved to Rochester where they associated with the local Quaker church and, until Lars's death in 1844, operated a way station for Norwegian immigrants, often providing food and lodging for as many as 100 people at one time.

LEWIS, JOHN TRAVERS

118. Clapson, Clive. JOHN TRAVERS LEWIS: AN IRISH HIGH CHURCHMAN IN CANADA WEST. *J. of the Can. Church Hist. Soc. (Canada) 1980 22(Oct): 17-31.*

John Travers Lewis (1825-1901) immigrated to Canada in 1850 from Ireland, where he had been educated at Trinity College, Dublin, and ordained by the Church of Ireland. In 1861 he was elected bishop of the new diocese of Ontario, where he remained though subsequently made metropolitan of Canada and, in 1894, archbishop. Lewis may have been elected bishop because of assumptions that he would, like most of the Irish clergy in Canada, support the Evangelical party. However, he quickly revealed an affinity for the Tractarians based upon their common respect for the church fathers and Caroline divines. In controversies during his episcopate, Lewis supported the episcopal constitution of the church, taught a high church view of the sacraments, and was sympathetic to moderate liturgical reform.

LINN, WILLIAM

119. Anderson, Philip J. WILLIAM LINN, 1752-1808: AMERICAN REVOLUTIONARY AND ANTI-JEFFERSONIAN. *J. of Presbyterian Hist. 1977 55(4): 381-394.*

The American Calvinist William Linn (1752-1808) was a typical American Revolutionary clergyman in identifying with the British all that was evil, with the Americans all that was righteous. Recognized as an excellent preacher as well as academician, after the Revolutionary War he held numerous influential pulpits and was associated with several schools. He wrote many books, including a life of George Washington. At first he hailed the French Revolution as an event that would extend God's activity in bringing liberty to the world, but the emerging irreligion turned him from it. Thomas Jefferson he accused of totally removing religion from politics, a course that could only lead to atheism. He thus stands as a poignant reminder of the perplexing dilemma which confronted so many of his clerical generation: the separation of church and state, and yet the perceived responsibility of the Church to keep government "Christian."

LINTON, MOSES LEWIS

120. Killoren, John J. THE DOCTOR'S SCRAPBOOK: A COLLABORATION OF LINTON AND DE SMET. *Gateway Heritage 1985-86 6(3): 2-9.*

A scrapbook owned by St. Louis University physician Moses Lewis Linton contains details of his friendship in 1850-72 with Jesuit missionary Pierre Jan De Smet. De Smet also recorded material about his missionary activities among Indians of the West and his observations about western fur traders. Also inserted into the scrapbook were 12 paintings by prominent St. Louis artists that adverted to De Smet's missionary work.

LIVINGSTON, WILLIAM

121. Mulder, John M. WILLIAM LIVINGSTON: PROPAGANDIST AGAINST EPISCOPACY. *J. of Presbyterian Hist. 1976 54(1): 83-104.*

William Livingston opposed the establishment of King's College (now Columbia University). He feared that a college under Episcopal influence would create an atmosphere of authoritarianism in all areas of the colony's life. Thus his opposition to an American episcopacy was not a sudden emergence. Livingston (1723-90) opposed bishops on the

Reformation principle of equality of clergy, as well as the complete separation of temporal and spiritual power. He portrayed the effort to establish an Anglican bishop in America as the ecclesiastical side of political imperialism. His battle against episcopacy played some role in formulating the ideology of the Revolution and attracting popular support. His anticlericalism also signaled a profound change in American religious life—the rise of the articulate layman.

LOPP, ELLEN KITTREDGE

122. Engerman, Jeanne. LETTERS FROM CAPE PRINCE OF WALES. A MISSION FAMILY IN NORTHWESTERN ALASKA 1892-1902.
Alaska Journal 1984 14(4): 33-41.

Describes the Alaska life of missionary Ellen Kittredge Lopp, who taught with her husband W. T. "Tom" Lopp in the government school at isolated Cape Prince of Wales, Alaska. Icebound nine months a year, Ellen Lopp wrote hundreds of letters to family and friends describing the everyday life at the mission. Besides teaching and preaching to the Eskimos there were the six children she bore to be cared for. Her letters reveal a powerful belief in her work however, and even after 10 years at the outpost, she had a strong reluctance to leave.

LOWRIE, JOHN C.

123. Waltmann, Henry G. JOHN C. LOWRIE AND PRESBYTERIAN INDIAN ADMINISTRATION, 1870-1882.
J. of Presbyterian Hist. 1976 54(2): 259-276.

John C. Lowrie (1808-1900) supervised the selection and counseling of church-nominated directors for as many as 11 western Indian agencies under the government's Indian "Peace Policy" during 1870-82. He leaned more toward Indian assimilation into American culture than toward cultural pluralism. As one who disparaged the Indians' heritage, leadership, and value systems, he was among those who contributed to their loss of identity and continuing social problems. Likewise, despite his advocacy of justice for the Indians, he did not think in terms of comprehensive equality for their race.

LYMAN, AMASA M.

124. Hefner, Loretta L. FROM APOSTLE TO APOSTATE: THE PERSONAL STRUGGLE OF AMASA MASON LYMAN.
Dialogue 1983 16(1): 90-104.

Amasa Mason Lyman was the only one of the first Twelve Apostles of the Church of Jesus Christ of Latter-Day Saints to be excommunicated for heresy, although two other apostles, Orson Pratt and Orson Hyde, had had to recant unacceptable doctrines. Recounts the history of his heresy and of his status in the church. He taught that man is perfectable by his own efforts and that Jesus Christ was nothing more than a good man. President Joseph F. Smith posthumously restored all Lyman's ordinances and blessings in 1909, on the grounds that his heresy was a symptom of mental illness.

LYMAN, AMY BROWN

125. Hefner, Loretta L. THIS DECADE WAS DIFFERENT: RELIEF SOCIETY'S SOCIAL SERVICES DEPARTMENT, 1919-1929.
Dialogue 1982 15(3): 64-73.

The decade was one of growing social responsibility for the Mormon Relief Society's Social Services Department. In 1917, Amy Brown Lyman, general secretary of the Relief Society General Board, was an official Utah delegate to the National Conference of Social Work, where she received Red Cross training. After more training in this area, she built up a strong corps of well-trained workers to fulfill the goals of the Social Services Department. They worked assiduously to provide health care, economic relief, and education to needy Utah families.

LYON, T. EDGAR

126. Lyon, T. Edgar. CHURCH HISTORIANS I HAVE KNOWN.
Dialogue 1978 11(4): 14-22.

The author reminisces about the lives and work of four Mormon historians who influenced his own development as a Mormon historian. B. H. Roberts, author of *The History of the Church* and president of the Church of the Latter Day Saints, attempted to break away from writing church history as propaganda. Andrew Jenson represents an earlier type of Mormon historian who collected historical information and documents, a chronicler striving for complete and accurate coverage. Similarly, A. William Lund, assistant historian in the Church Historian's Office, saw his responsibility as preserving documents and books, rather than making them accessible for use. Church historian Howard W. Hunter visited the author in Nauvoo, Illinois, and praised him for the concept of a church history that was people-oriented, not concerned only with abstractions.

M

MACQUEARY, HOWARD

127. Dennison, Mary S. HOWARD MACQUEARY: HERESY IN OHIO.
Hist. Mag. of the Protestant Episcopal Church 1980 49(2): 109-131.

Priest of St. Paul's Church (Episcopal), Canton, Ohio, the Reverend Howard MacQueary was representative of those clergy in the last quarter of the 19th century who were influenced by Darwinism and European biblical criticism emanating largely from Germany. After writing his only book, *The Evolution of Man and Christianity* (1890), he failed to heed the counsel of his ecclesiastical superior, Bishop Leonard, regarding his preaching. In 1891 he was charged with denying the virgin birth and Jesus's resurrection. His trial, the first of its kind in the Episcopal Church in America, was one of the numerous examples of the impact of European thought on America's churches. Found guilty, MacQueary left the Episcopal Church and later entered the Universalist Church.

MARSHALL, LOUIS

128. Rosenthal, Jerome C. A FRESH LOOK AT LOUIS
MARSHALL AND ZIONISM, 1900-1912.
Am. Jewish Arch. 1980 32(2): 109-118.

Louis Marshall, an influential constitutional lawyer, was a
devout Jew and eventually a Zionist. His background in
preimmigration New York City placed him in a Jewish elite
known for its neutrality to anti-Zionist leanings. Marshall's pro-
Zionist sentiments were seen in his letters to Nathan Straus,
Michael Leon, Solomon Schecter, and Jacob Schiff, as well as in
lectures to various Jewish groups and contributions to Herzl-
connected funds. By 1909 Marshall was sufficiently involved in
Zionist activities to cosponsor the construction of an
Agricultural Experiment Station in Palestine. Despite these
overtly pro-Zionist activities, Marshall in several letters
professed himself as neutral on the issue, claiming that his
actions and support were not politically motivated.

MARY JOSEPH, MOTHER

129 McKernan, Mary. MOTHER JOSEPH: PIONEER NUN.
Am. West 1981 18(5): 20-21.

Esther Pariseau (1823-1902), who learned carpentry from her
father, a Canadian carriage maker, entered the Montreal,
Quebec, convent of the Sisters of Charity of Providence and
soon became Mother Mary Joseph. In 1856, she was assigned to
duty in the Pacific Northwest. She constructed (literally as "fund
raiser, architect, estimator of materials, supervisor of
construction, and at times as carpenter, bricklayer, and wood-
carver") 11 hospitals, seven academies, two orphanages, four
homes for the aged and mentally ill, and five Indian schools. She
wore a hammer beside the rosary on her belt. Most of her
recognition has come posthumously from the American Institute
of Architects, the National Register of Historic Places, and the
state of Washington, which chose her as its second
representative in Statuary Hall at the nation's Capitol.

MATHER, COTTON

130. Hiner, N. Ray. COTTON MATHER AND HIS
FEMALE CHILDREN: NOTES ON THE RELATIONSHIP
BETWEEN PRIVATE EXPERIENCE AND PUBLIC
THOUGHT.
Journal of Psychohistory 1985 13(1): 33-49.

Cotton Mather, an eminent theologian, was thrice married, twice
widowed, and the father of 16 children, though only two
survived him. The high mortality rate among children in the
colonial period was, due to sickness and epidemics, common.
Mather tried to limit his bereavement by withholding affection
from his children but invariably loved them and grieved at their
loss. He wrote a number of pamphlets on how parents should
handle their grief and rear their children. His work strikes a
modern note in emphasizing the child's viewpoint.

MATHER, ELEAZER

131. Gura, Philip F. PREPARING THE WAY FOR
STODDARD: ELEAZER MATHER'S *SERIOUS
EXHORTATION* TO NORTHAMPTON.
New England Quarterly 1984 57(2): 240-249.

Eleazer Mather, brother of Increase Mather and the first minister
of Northampton, Massachusetts, has received little attention
from historians, probably because of his undistinguished record
as a clergyman and negligible influence on the development of
New England theology. In fact, Eleazer Mather only demands
attention because when he died in 1669 at the age of 32, he left
behind a community badly splintered by ecclesiastical disputes
and thereby set the terms of ecclesiastical debate for his
distinguished successors, Solomon Stoddard and Jonathan
Edwards. The chief evidence of the relationship between
Eleazer Mather and Stoddard lies in a collection of Mather's
sermons, which were posthumously published as *A Serious
Exhortation to the Present and Rising Generation.*

MATHER, MOSES

132. Noll, Mark A. MOSES MATHER (OLD CALVINIST) AND THE EVOLUTION OF EDWARDSEANISM. *Church Hist. 1980 49(3): 273-285.*

Moses Mather, an Old Light Calvinist, played an important role in the evolution of 19th-century Calvinism. Although Mather opposed the 18th-century Great Awakening, his thinking had much in common with ideas advanced during the Second Great Awakening. The author traces the line of descent from New England Puritanism to American Protestantism through the writings of Mather, especially during the first Awakening.

MATHIESON, ALEXANDER

133. Armstrong, Frederick H. THE REVEREND ALEXANDER MATHIESON OF MONTREAL: AN INQUIRY INTO PRESBYTERIAN PRACTICALITY. *J. of the Can. Church Hist. Soc. (Canada) 1981 23: 23-51.*

Alexander Mathieson (1795-1870) was one of the most prominent 19th-century Canadian Presbyterian ministers. Mathieson, a Scot and graduate of Glasgow College, arrived in Montreal in 1826 and, with one brief interruption, ministered at St. Andrew's Church from arrival until his death. Mathieson and his congregation reveal much about Scottish immigration, the relationship of religion to business success, and the practical implications of church disputes in the 19th century. Through his ministry and marriage to the daughter of a leading merchant, Mathieson became part of the Montreal establishment. His wealthy congregation erected the "Scotch Cathedral" in Montreal and became the church of the most successful Scots of the city. Mathieson was active in forming the Synod of the Presbyterian Church in Connection with the Church of Scotland in 1831, served twice as its moderator, and insisted on continued connection with the Scottish state church after the Disruption of 1843, though this resulted in a Canadian schism. Mathieson resisted efforts to reunify the church, and the congregation refused to enter the Union of 1875.

MATTHEWS, MARK ALLISON

134. Russell, C. Allyn. MARK ALLISON MATTHEWS: SEATTLE FUNDAMENTALIST AND CIVIC REFORMER. *J. of Presbyterian Hist. 1979 57(4): 446-466.*

Concentrates on the social concerns of Mark Allison Matthews (1867-1940), pastor of the First Presbyterian Church, Seattle, Washington. He was a strange mixture of biblical fundamentalism and social reform. Under him his congregation became the largest Presbyterian church in the United States. He was an intense critic of religious liberalism at the time of the modernist-fundamentalist controversy, yet participated actively in the civic and political life of Seattle. Describes in detail his pulpit ability, executive acumen, and fundamentalist theology.

135. Soden, Dale E. MARK ALLISON MATTHEWS: SEATTLE'S MINISTER REDISCOVERED. *Pacific Northwest Q. 1983 74(2): 50-58.*

Mark Allison Matthews (1867-1940) left his Southern Populist roots, migrated west, and by 1902 accepted the pastorate at Seattle's First Presbyterian Church. Already a strong convert to the Social Gospel and Progressive movements, he immediately involved himself in reformist actions for the city. Matthews's uncompromising efforts to clean up the city eventually led him to a reactionary approach that embraced the tenets of nativism, anti-Semitism, anti-unionism, and anti-liberal theology.

MATTHEWS, ROBERT ("MATTHIAS THE PROPHET")

136. McDade, Thomas M. MATTHIAS, PROPHET WITHOUT HONOR. *New-York Hist. Soc. Q. 1978 62(4): 311-334.*

Among the many religious eccentrics to appear in the 1820's and '30's in New York was Robert Matthews, who had a brief (1828-35) but newsworthy career in New York City. Known as Matthias the Prophet, he was able to dazzle a small group of people, members of the so-called Retrenchment Society, some of whom had money and property. Matthias controlled the group with a mixture of piety, sex, and an ability to win over reasonably sane people, particularly women. Finally, after some wife-swapping and similar activities, one husband died in mysterious circumstances. Murder probably had been done, but not enough evidence existed to indict Matthias. Nevertheless, his hold on the followers began to weaken. By mid-1835, the movement collapsed and Matthias disappeared from sight. The only person to emerge unscathed was a black woman named Isabella Van Wagenen who later became justly famous as Sojourner Truth.

MCCALLA, DANIEL

137. Briceland, Alan V. DANIEL McCALLA, 1748-1809: NEW SIDE REVOLUTIONARY AND JEFFERSONIAN. *J. of Presbyterian Hist. 1978 56(3): 252-269.*

Daniel McCalla (1748-1809) was born in the midst of a Presbyterian schism. Wh1le he never figured as a major factor in his church or country, his life touched and made contributions to several important historical processes. As an academy teacher, he brought education to students with limited educational opportunities; as a chaplain, he aided the cause of the American Revolution; as a Presbyterian, he fought to establish the principle of separation of church and state; as a scholar, he published essays to enlighten and reform; as one committed to democracy, he enlisted his pen in the cause of electing Thomas Jefferson.

MCCORMICK, VINCENT A.

138. Hennesey, James. AMERICAN JESUIT IN WARTIME ROME: THE DIARY OF VINCENT A. McCORMICK, S.J., 1942-1945. *Mid-America 1974 56(1): 32-55.*

Brooklyn-born Vincent A. McCormick, a Jesuit since 1903, served in Rome from 1934 until after World War II. Among his few personal papers he left several small notebook diaries reflecting his life in Rome during 1942-45. While much of the material involves internal Jesuit matters, many entries refer to contemporary church and political affairs. Some critical remarks are directed toward the Holy See's stance toward the Fascist countries, and secular matters such as the Church's expressed concern at the damage to the San Lorenzo Basilica being more pronounced than its abhorrence of the loss of life from a bombing attack. His own deep loyalty to the Pope and the Church caused him much anguish, some of which is clearly expressed in the diary.

MCDONOUGH, DAVID

139. Murray, Andrew E. BRIGHT DELUSION: PRESBYTERIANS AND AFRICAN COLONIZATION. *J. of Presbyterian Hist. 1980 58(3): 224-237.*

The basic flaw of the American Colonization Society (ACS) was its effort to ease the troubled consciences of white Americans while ignoring the needs and desires of black people. Points out the paradox in the life of David McDonough, an American slave whose master wanted him trained for leadership in Africa. Details the many frustrations McDonough confronted in his preparation to be a physician, due to prejudice. The ACS did not meet the needs of all blacks. For McDonough and others, colonization attempted to solve the problems of white oppressors by requiring the victims of that oppression to make major sacrifices. Covers ca. 1940-50.

MEAD, GEORGE HERBERT

140. Karier, Clarence J. IN SEARCH OF SELF IN A MORAL UNIVERSE: A CRITIQUE OF THE LIFE AND THOUGHT OF GEORGE HERBERT MEAD. *J. of the Hist. of Ideas 1984 45(1): 153-161.*

A general assessment of the social psychology of George Herbert Mead that stresses the importance of his religious background and interests. Mead's parents were closely tied to Protestantism and Mead himself considered a career in the clergy for a while. Even after committing to a profession that emphasized humanistic and scientific perspectives, he endeavored to keep Christian beliefs or their sociological and psychological surrogates vital in the modern, increasingly alienated world. For Mead, every society implicitly contains a moral ideal and the functional role of this sort of ideal in the assimilation and realization of the "self." His thought continually slipped between the descriptive and the prescriptive.

MENNINGER, KARL A.

141. Pruyser, Paul W. RELIGIO MEDICI: KARL A
MENNINGER, CALVINISM AND THE PRESBYTERIAN
CHURCH.
J. of Presbyterian Hist. 1981 59(1): 59-72.

In 1930 Karl A. Menninger of Topeka, Kansas, became
nationally known when he published *The Human Mind.* In the
second edition (1937) he added a section on "Religious
Application," assisted by religious experts. Raised under the
religious tutelage of his mother and the First Presbyterian
Church of Topeka, Menninger developed a great interest in
religion, and in Calvinism in particular. The latter contributed to
his sense of vocation and his desire to explore. His marriage to
Presbyterian Jeanetta Lyle called attention to a cornerstone
conviction about human personality: the instinctual given of
love. His Calvinism enabled him to align himself with Freud's
thesis that a death instinct must be postulated to account for
otherwise puzzling phenomena of self-destructiveness. As Elder
in the church, Menninger has taken his ecclesiastical
responsibilities as seriously as his religiously personal ones.

MILLIGAN, JAMES

142. Roth, Randolph A. THE FIRST RADICAL
ABOLITIONISTS: THE REVEREND JAMES MILLIGAN
AND THE REFORMED PRESBYTERIANS OF VERMONT.
New England Q. 1982 55(4): 540-563.

In 1819 Reverend James Milligan, pastor of the Reformed
Presbyterian Church of Ryegate, Vermont, stood alone as an
advocate of the immediate, unconditional abolition of slavery
and the full integration of blacks into American society. Traces
Milligan's life from his birth in Scotland in 1785 to his coming
to Ryegate in 1816; the history of his congregation, the Scottish
"Covenanters" of the Upper Connecticut River Valley, and their
antagonists, the Reformed and Associate Presbyterian Seceders;
and Milligan's efforts, particularly his *Narrative* (1819), to
thwart any attempts by the Seceders and Covenanters to unite
and settle their doctrinal differences.

MOBLEY, HARDY (FAMILY)

143. Richardson, Joe M. "LABOR IS REST TO ME HERE IN THIS THE LORD'S VINEYARD": HARDY MOBLEY, BLACK MISSIONARY DURING RECONSTRUCTION. *Southern Studies 1983 22(1): 5-20.*

Hardy Mobley, born a slave in Georgia, later bought his freedom and moved to New York to be educated and become a Congregational minister. After the Civil War, he labored in Georgia, Missouri, and Louisiana as a missionary and teacher for the American Missionary Association. On a meager salary, he and his daughters taught, visited the sick, tended the dying, and helped fellow blacks in every way possible. Despite his selfless activities, Mobley was eventually dismissed from the association for political reasons.

MOCZYGEMBA, LEOPOLD

144. Baker, T. Lindsay. THE REVEREND LEOPOLD MOCZYGEMBA, PATRIARCH OF POLONIA. *Polish Am. Studies 1984 41(1): 66-109.*

Portrays Father Leopold Moczygemba as being more than the reputed founder of the first permanent Polish-American settlement in Panna Marya, Texas. Credits Father Moczygemba with the origination of Franciscan churches and friaries in the eastern United States, the establishment of several Roman Catholic parishes, helping found the Polish Roman Catholic Union (a fraternal lodge), and helping found the Polish Seminary in Orchard Lake, Michigan.

MOLLOY, MARY ALOYSIUS

145. Kennelly, Karen. MARY MOLLOY: WOMEN'S COLLEGE FOUNDER.
Stuhler, Barbara and Kreuter, Gretchen, ed.
Women of Minnesota: Selected Biographical Essays (St. Paul: Minnesota Historical Society Press, 1977): 116-135.

Born on 14 June 1880, in Sandusky, Ohio, Mary Aloysia Molloy grew up as the only child of Irish Catholic immigrant parents. In an age when few women attended college, Molloy earned her way through Ohio State University and graduated, in 1903, with more honors than anyone else up to that time. She went on to earn a master's degree and election to Phi Beta Kappa at Ohio State. In 1907 she earned her doctorate at Cornell. That same year, she began her career as a Catholic college educator in Winona, Minnesota, when she accepted a job with the Franciscan Sisters who, under the leadership of Sister Leo Tracy, were creating the liberal arts College of St. Teresa. The two women persevered and successfully established and administered the new collegiate institution for Catholic lay and religious women. Molloy was unique as the lay dean of a Catholic college, but in 1922 she became a nun, Sister Mary Aloysius Molloy, and in 1928 became the college president. As an educator, Molloy worked hard to improve the quality of women's education, wrestled with the unique problems of Catholic colleges, and carefully oversaw the development of her own school. By 1946, when she retired, the college was a firmly established institution producing outstanding graduate women. One of the last among the heroic generation of founders of Minnesota women's colleges, Molloy died on 27 September 1954.

MORGAN, WILLIAM

146. Hancock, Harold B., ed. WILLIAM MORGAN'S AUTOBIOGRAPHY AND DIARY: LIFE IN SUSSEX COUNTY, 1780-1857.
Delaware Hist. 1980 19(1): 39-52.

Publishes the diary and excerpts from the autobiography of a Methodist Protestant minister residing in Sussex County, Delaware. The diary and autobiography relate William Morgan's childhood and education, his conversion experience, revivals, descriptions of church services and political rallies, his involvement with the Sons of Temperance, Sussex County social life, medical history of the region, and farming practices. As a preacher, farmer, and physician, Morgan touched the lives and interests of most inhabitants of the county.

147. Hancock, Harold B., ed. WILLIAM MORGAN'S AUTOBIOGRAPHY AND DIARY: LIFE IN SUSSEX COUNTY, 1780-1857. PART II.
Delaware Hist. 1980 19(2): 106-126.

Continued from a previous article. Entries from William Morgan's diary from 1829 until Morgan's death in 1857 recount the effort to introduce silk culture in Delaware, July 4th celebrations, the author's meetings with (and assessments of) various religious figures (principally Methodists) and politicians in Delaware, revivals, the Millerite movement, fishing, sharp dealings at the Cannon Ferry, shipbuilding and sailing, and Sussex County social life, medical practices, and farming.

MORGENTHAU, HENRY, SR.

148. Tuchman, Barbara W. THE ASSIMILATIONIST DILEMMA: AMBASSADOR MORGENTHAU'S STORY. *Commentary 1977 63(5): 58-62.*

In 1914 Henry Morgenthau, Sr., then US Ambassador to Turkey, arranged for financial aid to the Jewish colony in Palestine, enabling it to survive and preserving it for eventual Jewish statehood. Yet in 1918 he resigned as president of the Free Synagogue, when its Rabbi, Stephen S. Wise, led a delegation to the White House to support the Zionist homeland, and in 1921 he wrote an article stating his strong opposition to Zionism. Not until after the Holocaust, when he was in his 80's, did Morgenthau acknowledge that he had misread history. Assimilation into American life was his ideal, assimilation meaning acceptance as Jews, not absorption into Christianity. The Western Democracies did not function according to his ideal and the horrors of the Holocaust turned many assimilationists into supporters of the Jewish State.

MORIARTY, PATRICK E.

149. George, Joseph, Jr. VERY REV. DR. PATRICK E. MORIARTY, OSA., PHILADELPHIA'S FENIAN SPOKESMAN. *Pennsylvania Hist. 1981 48(3): 221-233.*

Father Patrick E. Moriarty, an Irish Augustinian priest, served in Philadelphia from 1839 until his death in 1875. A noted orator, Moriarty was ordered by his bishop to leave Philadelphia for a time, after he lashed out at nativists who burned his church and rectory in 1844. Later, in 1864, Bishop James F. Wood suspended Moriarty for disobeying him by making a speech, sounding Fenian in tone and sponsorship, "What Right Has England to Rule Ireland?" The English American bishop and the eloquent Irishman reconciled later that year.

MOTT, LUCRETIA

150. Greene, Dana. QUAKER FEMINISM: THE CASE OF LUCRETIA MOTT.
Pennsylvania Hist. 1981 48(2): 143-154.

Lucretia Mott's (d. 1880) commitment to feminism and to various reform movements grew out of her religious experience as a member of the Society of Friends, where she learned that women are equal to men. Her quest for religious self-perfection led her first to abolitionism and then to other reforms.

MULLINS, EDGAR YOUNG

151. Stubblefield, Jerry M. THE ECUMENICAL IMPACT OF E. Y. MULLINS.
J. of Ecumenical Studies 1980 17(2): 94-102.

Edgar Young Mullins (1860-1928), prominent Southern Baptist minister and president of Southern Baptist Seminary and the Baptist World Alliance, evaluated the ecumenical movement in a book entitled *The Axioms of Religion.* He felt that ecumenical negotiations operated by two methods: addition and subtraction, i.e. either finding a commonly held position and asking churches to unite because of that, or paring down positions to the lowest common denominator in order to foster agreement. If the latter method was to be favored, he outlined six axioms which Baptists would hold as minimal for the true faith: the sovereignty of God, equal access to God, equal privileges in the church, human responsibility, the Golden Rule, and a free church in a free state.

MUNDELEIN, GEORGE

152. Kantowicz, Edward R. CARDINAL MUNDELEIN OF CHICAGO AND THE SHAPING OF TWENTIETH-CENTURY AMERICAN CATHOLICISM.
J. of Am. Hist. 1981 68(1): 52-68.

George Cardinal Mundelein of Chicago (d. 1939) was one of several American-born but Roman-trained bishops who, as "consolidating bishops," centralized the Church's structure and tied American Catholicism more closely to Rome. Mundelein and other 20th-century bishops brought much-needed recognition to the American Catholic Church and gave its members pride and confidence. Mundelein was famous for his administrative talents, patriotism, political influence, and princely style.

MURPHY, EDGAR GARDNER

153. Compton, Stephen C. EDGAR GARDNER MURPHY AND THE CHILD LABOR MOVEMENT.
Hist. Mag. of the Protestant Episcopal Church 1983 52(2): 181-194.

The strength of the child labor movement was greatly enhanced by Edgar Gardner Murphy (b. 1869), an Episcopal priest who has been credited with having done more than any other person to awaken the South to the wrongs of child labor. Murphy was greatly influenced by his mentor at the University of the South, Wiliam Porcher DuBose, who emphasized unity of persons to God, to themselves, and to each other as the key to life. Murphy was quite active in race and education in Alabama before he became involved in the child labor movement. Traces Murphy's role in getting the Child Labor Act enacted in Alabama in 1907, which ended the horrible conditions under which children worked in Southern cotton mills.

N

NEISSER, GEORGE

154. Frank, Albert H. GEORGE NEISSER: AN EARLY MORAVIAN HISTORIAN.
Tr. of the Moravian Hist. Soc. 1979 23(2): 1-11.

Surveys the known details of the life of George Neisser (1715-84), a Moravian Brethren, from his early lay work in Georgia to his later pastoral work in eastern Pennsylvania and New York.

He was sympathetic to the American revolutionary cause, was a student of Moravian hymnology, and compiled biographical, genealogical, and historical information on his church and its members.

NEWTON, JOSEPH FORT

155. Leonard, Bill J. JOSEPH FORT NEWTON: ECCLESIASTICAL NOMAD. *Hist. Mag. of the Protestant Episcopal Church 1981 50(3): 299-311.*

Joseph Fort Newton (1876-1950) began his ministerial career in the Southern Baptist Church. He then identified with the nonsectarian movement and later became pastor of the Liberal Christian Church of Cedar Rapids. From there he went to London's City Temple. Returning to the United States in 1919, he accepted the pulpit of New York's Universalist Church of the Divine Paternity. In 1925 he converted to the Protestant Episcopal Church, serving parishes in the Philadelphia area until his death. Emphasizes his ecumenical concerns, broad church outlook, mysticism, publications, and preaching.

NICHOLSON, FRANCIS

156. McCully, Bruce T. GOVERNOR FRANCIS NICHOLSON, PATRON *PAR EXCELLENCE* OF RELIGION AND LEARNING IN COLONIAL AMERICA. *William and Mary Q. 1982 39(2): 310-333.*

Examines the role of Francis Nicholson that historians have ignored—his patronage of religion, education, libraries, botany, and cartography. Outlines Nicholson's benefactions as governor (or lieutenant governor) of Maryland, Virginia, South Carolina, New York, and Nova Scotia, as well as during his travels. As a patron of the Anglican Church, he also did much to promote the church in New England, of which he was the "nursing Father." He was influential in establishing schools, and he donated to the libraries of learned societies. He aided the Royal Society in collecting American flora, and experimented in gardening himself. Nicholson was motivated by quest for status and altruism.

NOLAN, JAMES L.

157. Neuerburg, Norman. THE ANGEL ON THE CLOUD, OR "ANGLO-AMERICAN MYOPIA" REVISITED: A DISCUSSION OF THE WRITINGS OF JAMES L. NOLAN. *Southern California Q. 1980 62(1): 1-48.*

Assesses the work of James L. Nolan in analyzing California mission art, especially his criticisms of Anglo-American misperceptions of Catholic religious figures and decorations in mission churches. Nolan's view of this art as part of a total artistic environment is generally accepted, but his research suffers from numerous minor errors, a narrow focus, and omissions, particularly in his failure to consult Mexican and Spanish scholarship. Moreover, Nolan's interpretations of the implications of mission art would probably have been lost on the Indian neophytes despite the best efforts of the missionaries. Nolan should expand the scope of his own research to include comparative analysis with the church art of Hispanic and European countries, not just contrasting California mission art with Anglo-American views.

NORRIS, DEBORAH

158. Derounian, Kathryn Zabelle. "A DEAR DEAR FRIEND": SIX LETTERS FROM DEBORAH NORRIS TO SALLY WISTER, 1778-1779. *Pennsylvania Mag. of Hist. and Biog. 1984 108(4): 487-516.*

Describes the lives of two Quaker women whose lives diverged after their adolescent friendship. Reproduces 6 letters in the Norris-Wister correspondence which reveal an emphasis on the theme of friendship over public issues.

NORRIS, J. FRANK

159. Measures, Royce. J. FRANK NORRIS: A FORERUNNER OF THE NEW RIGHT. *Fides et Hist. 1982 15(1): 61-70.*

Analyzes the life of the controversial and enigmatic Texas Baptist minister, J. Frank Norris. A fundamentalist firebrand, Norris distinguished himself at Fort Worth's First Baptist

Church where he preached for 43 years, much to the consternation of mainline Baptists. Through his influential newspaper, the *Baptist Standard,* Norris attacked the evils of racetrack betting and succeeded in getting the practice outlawed in 1908. His greatest political triumph came in 1928 when he waged a vigorous partisan attack against the Catholic Democratic presidential candidate, Al Smith, and helped in getting staunchly Democratic Texas to go for Hoover. His influence on the modern New Right religious movement is obscure and tangential at best.

O

OCCOM, SAMUEL

160. Peyer, Bernd. SAMSON OCCOM: MOHEGAN MISSIONARY AND WRITER OF THE 18TH CENTURY. *Am. Indian Q. 1982 6(3-4): 208-217.*

Describes the life of the first Native American English language author, Samuel Occom, who wrote religious tracts during the last quarter of the 18th century. Occom, a Mohegan, was minister to several Indian congregations and championed Indian causes despite being a Christian. Occom was discriminated against because he was an Indian. He should be remembered as the "father" of modern Native American literature.

OLDHAM, WILLIAM FITZJAMES

161. Doraisamy, Theodore R. RESCUING THE OLDHAM LEGEND. *Methodist Hist. 1979 18(1): 61-65.*

William Fitzjames Oldham (1854-1937) was the founder of Methodism in Singapore in 1885 and missionary bishop of the Singapore-Philippines area, 1904-12. Urges that his accomplishments be researched and written rather than allowed to sink into oblivion.

OLIVER, EDMUND HENRY

162. Barnhart, Gordon. THE PRAIRIE PASTOR: E. H. OLIVER.
Saskatchewan History (Canada) 1984 37(3): 81-94.

Edmund Henry Oliver was a Canadian clergyman, educator, and statesman. Educated in both history and theology, Oliver began his professional teaching career at Toronto's McMaster University in 1905 and from there moved westward to Saskatoon, Saskatchewan, where he was founder of Presbyterian Theological College in 1913. He worked through both clerical and secular spheres to help bring spiritual leadership to growing western Canada and to help ease the economic and political tensions between eastern and western Canada. In 1930, Oliver became moderator of the United Church of Canada, and he effectively used his position to further cooperation in a divided Canada during the following years' drought and depression.

OSGOOD, THADDEUS

163. Millar, W. P. J. THE REMARKABLE REV. THADDEUS OSGOOD: A STUDY IN THE EVANGELICAL SPIRIT IN THE CANADAS.
Social Hist. (Canada) 1977 10(19): 59-76.

Traces career of nondenominational traveling preacher Thaddeus Osgood (1775-1852) in Canada after 1807. He attempted to stimulate a vast spiritual awakening. He believed such an awakening could not be left to faith alone, but must be assisted by such means as day and Sunday schools, education of Indians, temperance movements, sabbatarianism, organization of tract societies, and an attack on urban poverty and vice. By the 1820's he met strong resistance from the sources of denominationalism. By 1835 he had narrowed his activities to the moral improvement of the urban poor, especially children.

OTTOLENGHE, JOSEPH SOLOMON

164. VanHorne, John C. JOSEPH SOLOMON OTTOLENGHE (CA. 1711-1775): CATECHIST TO THE

NEGROES, SUPERINTENDENT OF THE SILK CULTURE, AND PUBLIC SERVANT IN COLONIAL GEORGIA. *Pro. of the Am. Phil. Soc. 1981 125(5): 398-409.*

Joseph Solomon Ottolenghe was an Italian-born Jew who converted to Christianity. After residing in England for several years, he went to Georgia as a catechist to the Negroes under the joint auspices of the Society for the Propagation of the Gospel in Foreign Parts and the Associates of Dr. Bray. This commission began in 1751 and ended in 1761. In the meantime he had become involved in the attempts of the colony to manufacture silk, since he had worked in the silk industry in Italy. He was involved successfully in this enterprise from 1751 to 1764. From 1755 to 1766 he sat for Savannah in the Georgia House of Commons, where he introduced a large number of bills that were adopted. If his rise to prominence can be partly attributed to the social mobility that characterized colonial Georgia, it was equally due to his own ambition and drive, forces that impelled him to act for the good in many spheres of the colony's life.

P

PAINE, THOMAS

165. Kashatus, William C., III. THOMAS PAINE: A QUAKER REVOLUTIONARY. *Quaker Hist. 1984 73(2): 38-61.*

Thomas Paine's writings, 1776-77, reflect William Penn's and other Quakers' influence with respect to loyalty to legitimate government, greater avoidance of violence than Lockean "commonwealth" political theory or Enlightenment rationalism proposed, a millennial spirit, and plain language. Paine was raised a Quaker in Thetford, England, and was caught up in Whig republican agitation as a customs officer in Lewes, 1768-74. In Philadelphia, 1774-77, he sympathized with Quakers supporting violent revolution, who were eventually disowned by orthodox Quakers. As editor of the *Pennsylvania Magazine*, 1774-76, and as aide-de-camp to General Nathaniel Greene (also of Quaker background), Paine's Quaker heritage appeared, too, in his antislavery, antidueling, and feminist sentiments.

PAPERMASTER, BENJAMIN

166. Papermaster, Isadore. A HISTORY OF NORTH
DAKOTA JEWRY AND THEIR PIONEER RABBI.
*Western States Jewish Hist. Q. 1977 10(1): 74-89; 1978 10(2):
170-184, (3): 266-283.*

Part I. Rabbi Benjamin Papermaster was born in Lithuania in
1860. He agreed to come to America in 1890 to serve a party of
immigrants as its religious leader and teacher. He settled in
Grand Forks, North Dakota, amid a growing congregation of
Jews from the Ukraine, Rumania, Poland, and Germany. Most
of the Jews at that time were peddlers who mortgaged their
houses and wagons to build the first synagogue. Rabbi
Papermaster was enthusiastic about America; his letters to his
family in Lithuania brought many relatives to join him. Grand
Forks was considered a boom town because of the building of
the Great Northern Railway. The influx of eastern capital helped
the development of Jewish merchants. *Part II.* Until the turn of
the century, Rabbi Papermaster of Grand Forks was the only
rabbi serving Jews in all f North Dakota and western Minnesota.
Jewish families who started as peddlers became prosperous
enough to move out to towns and villages where they opened
small shops and stores. Other families followed the Great
Northern Railway along its branch lines toward the Canadian
border. In Grand Forks, the Jewish community established a
modern Hebrew school, a Ladies' Aid Society, and a burial
society. *Part III.* The city of Grand Forks, at the urging of Rabbi
Papermaster, acquired a sanitary meat slaughtering facility with
a special department for kosher beef. Rabbi Papermaster
maintained an active interest in local politics, generally favoring
the Republican Party but supporting Democrats when he knew
them to be good men. Although a member of a Zionist
organization, he worried about the antireligious character of the
modern movement. During World War I he urged Jewish youths
to their patriotic duty of joining the American armed forces.
Rabbi Papermaster died on 24 September 1934.

PARHAM, CHARLES F.

167. Goff, James R., Jr. CHARLES F. PARHAM AND HIS
ROLE IN THE DEVELOPMENT OF THE PENTECOSTAL
MOVEMENT: A REEVALUATION.
Kansas History 1984 7(3): 226-237.

Asserts the importance of Charles F. Parham of Topeka in the development of the pentecostal or apostolic faith movement. Because many scholars and pentecostal theologians emphasize the divine origins of pentecostalism, they unfortunately overlook the role of its early leaders. A review of Parham's life leads to the conclusion that he may well have been pentecostalism's first prophet and greatest leader, since he was the first to develop the idea that speaking in tongues was a baptism of the Holy Spirit. Parham embodied the many complexities of the pentecostal movement: he was theologically daring yet fundamentalistic, often anti-intellectual yet an advocate of Christian education and the formation of new schools.

PAYNE, DANIEL ALEXANDER

168. Noon, Thomas R. DANIEL PAYNE AND THE LUTHERANS. *Concordia Hist. Inst. Q. 1980 53(2): 51-69.*

Discusses the Reverend Doctor Daniel Alexander Payne (1811-93) whose accomplishments include being the first black college president of Wilberforce University (1863-76) and most likely the first black ordained Lutheran pastor in the United States (1839), focusing on his less than seven years involvement with the Lutheran Church due to his redirection to the African Methodist Episcopal Church.

PAYZANT, JOHN

169. Cuthbertson, B. C. REV. JOHN PAYZANT: HENRY ALLINE'S SUCCESSOR. *Nova Scotia Hist. Soc. Collections (Canada) 1980 40: 57-80.*

John Payzant (1749-1834) is regarded as Henry Alline's successor "who attempted to guide Nova Scotian New Lightism by giving it both spiritual and organizational direction after Alline's death." Born in England and educated by the Jesuits in Quebec, Payzant was "awakened" at the age of 20, then befriended by Alline. He served churches in Falmouth, Newport, Horton, and Liverpool. The career of this preacher parallels closely the history of the New Lights. This sect, however, lacked an organization basis which Payzant attempted to provide primarily through discipline.

PEABODY, ENDICOTT

170. Kintrea, Frank. "OLD PEABO" AND THE SCHOOL. *Am. Heritage 1980 31(6): 98-105.*

The Reverend Endicott Peabody (1857-1944), an Episcopalian, founded Groton School in Groton, Massachusetts, in 1884 and remained its master until he retired in 1940. During his time, the school achieved fame as a preserve of wealth and privilege. Peabody's acceptance of biblical infallibility and his belief in hard work led to a dogma of "muscular Christianity" at the school.

PENN, WILLIAM

171. Morgan, Edmund S. THE WORLD OF WILLIAM PENN. *Pro. of the Am. Phil. Soc. 1983 127(5): 291-315.*

William Penn made his life a testimony against the world in which he lived. He was not content to acquiesce to the social order. Penn wanted to change the world immediately, and he left his mark on it because he did not reject as much of the world as he seemed to; he knew how the world worked and he was prepared to work within its terms. Discusses aspects of Penn's personality as a Protestant, a gentleman, and an Englishman. In regard to Pennsylvania, Penn expected too much both of himself and of those he persuaded to settle. While Quaker spiritual perfection meant self-denial, he was not ready to deny himself privileges and rights that he thought were his perquisites as founder. Further, his colonists seemed equally unwilling to deny themselves anything.

PHIPS, WILLIAM

172. Gura, Philip F. COTTON MATHER'S *LIFE OF PHIPS:* "A VICE WITH THE VIZARD OF VERTUE UPON IT." *New England Q. 1977 50(3): 440-457.*

Sketches Sir William Phips's (1651-95) career and shows how Cotton Mather's 1697 biography of the governor of Massachusetts was written to justify the actions of his close associate. Mather's commendation of Phips's ambition, patriotism, and rise in society contrasts with the earlier Puritan stress on piety, service to the Lord, and acceptance of one's place in society. Mather's defense marked a shift from a personal piety to public patriotism as the standard of leadership. Facing a crisis in both personal and community terms, Mather hoped that by justifying Phips's actions and reminding people of his ties to Phips, he could both instill in society some of its lost Puritan fervor and bolster his own position as its leader.

PORTIER, MICHAEL

173. Lipscomb, Oscar H. ALABAMA'S FIRST BISHOP HAD A SENSE OF HUMOR. *Alabama Rev. 1982 35(1): 3-13.*

A consideration of the life and works of Bishop Michael Portier, French-born first Catholic Bishop of Alabama and Florida, with special emphasis on his light-hearted good humor. Portier came to the New World in 1826 without anticipations as to the roughness of the life he would find there. He suffered his share of illnesses and privations, none of which dampened either his ardor or his humor. He traveled considerably during his later years, always without pomp and ostentation, dying in Mobile in an infirmary he had founded.

PRANDO, PETER PAUL

174. Engh, Michael E. PETER PAUL PRANDO, S. J., "APOSTLE OF THE CROWS." *Montana 1984 34(4): 24-31.*

Peter Paul Prando helped found St. Xavier's Mission on the Crow Reservation in 1887. He had previously been assigned to missions among the Blackfoot, Flathead, and Northern Cheyenne Indians. A trained linguist, Prando learned the Blackfoot and Cheyenne languages, compiled a Crow grammar and a Crow-English dictionary, and transcribed and translated Crow accounts of their traditions and beliefs. To encourage tribal self-sufficiency he energetically promoted the Crow Irrigation Project. An amateur photographer, Prando left a significant pictorial record of the Crow tribe's painful adjustment to reservation life.

PROPST, MISSOURI POWELL

175. Propst, Nell Brown. VOICE FROM THE FRONTIER. *Methodist Hist. 1982 20(2): 51-59.*

Missouri Powell Propst, born in Alabama and a daughter of a sometime Methodist minister, came with her husband to northeastern Colorado in 1874 to participate in taming the frontier. She helped to organize the first Methodist Episcopal Church, South in the area and later tried to serve in a meaningful way with the congregation of the northern Methodist Episcopal Church. When she found that women were used in a very limited way in the church, she sent, in 1891, an article in protest to the *Christian Advocate.* Her article, which was not accepted, is printed here.

R

RAND, SILAS TERTIUS

176. Marshall, Mortimer Villiers. SILAS TERTIUS RAND AND HIS MICMAC DICTIONARY. *Nova Scotia Hist. Q. (Canada) 1975 5(4): 391-410.*

Silas Tertius Rand (1810-89) was a self-taught linguist, Baptist pastor, and missionary to the Micmac Indians of Nova Scotia. He collected Indian legends, translated the Bible into Micmac and Maliseet, compiled a Micmac dictionary, gathered a great amount of linguistic and philological data on the Micmac and Maliseet languages, and lectured extensively on Indian languages, customs, and traditions, including ethnological and anthropological topics. Though he was without formal schooling, his philological accomplishments were widely recognized in university circles.

RANSOM, REVERDY C.

177. Morris, Calvin S. REVERDY RANSOM, THE SOCIAL GOSPEL AND RACE. *J. of Religious Thought 1984 41(1): 7-21.*

The Social Gospel movement had a substantial influence on black religious leader Reverdy C. Ransom, who became a proponent of socialism as a means of improving the low economic position of blacks in the United States and Africa, though he rejected the Social Gospeler's assertion that heredity, not environment, was responsible for the black worker's plight.

RAYMOND, ALMIRA AND WILLIAM WAKEMAN

178. Freeman, Olga, ed. ALMIRA RAYMOND LETTERS, 1840-1880.
Oregon Hist. Q. 1984 85(3): 291-303.

Almira Raymond and her husband, William Wakeman Raymond, sailed from New York in October 1839 and arrived at Fort Vancouver in June 1840, along with other Methodist missionaries for the Pacific Northwest. From their mission stations on the Willamette River and at Tansey Point, she wrote letters to her family, describing their work with the Indians, the physical hardships, illnesses, and loneliness. Later letters speak of their success as Clatsop County dairy farmers and William Raymond's work as an Indian agent.

RAYMOND, ELIZA RUGGLES

179. Cousins, Leone B. WOMAN OF THE YEAR: 1842.
Nova Scotia Hist. Q. (Canada) 1976 6(4): 349-374.

Eliza Ruggles Raymond of Nova Scotia married a minister who was a missionary to escaped slaves and who eventually had a mission on Sherbro Island; she aided slaves on slaving vessels, accompanied her husband to Africa, and defended wrongly accused slaves against imprisonment, 1839-50.

REED, ISAAC

180. Thompson, Donald E. and Sylvester, Lorna Lutes, ed. THE AUTOBIOGRAPHY OF ISAAC REED, FRONTIER MISSIONARY.
Indiana Mag. of Hist. 1982 78(3): 193-214.

Isaac Reed served as a Presbyterian missionary and teacher in Indiana, Kentucky, Illinois, and Ohio from the late 1820's until the mid-1850's. This portion of his diary covers 1828-39 and 1844-45 and concentrates on his activities of founding many churches, teaching several frontier schools, and working for the establishment of many small colleges and seminaries in these states. The diary entries emphasize his professional life and the recurring physical ailments he suffered.

RHOADS, THOMAS

181. Davies, J. Kenneth. THOMAS RHOADS, FORGOTTEN MORMON PIONEER OF 1846. *Nebraska Hist. 1983 64(1): 81-95.*

Thomas Rhoads was a prominent Mormon pioneer, whose contributions though well-known among Mormon leaders were minimized in an effort to retain control in Utah. Rhoads's monetary contributions and role in the development of mining were ignored because Mormon leaders did not wish to focus outside attention on the possibility for wealth in the Utah territory.

RICHARDS, GEORGE WARREN

182. Romig, Michael C. GEORGE WARREN RICHARDS: ARCHITECT OF CHURCH UNION. *J. of Presbyterian Hist. 1977 55(1): 74-99.*

Discusses the contributions of George Warren Richards (1869-1957) to church union. Examines three areas of Richards' life and thought: the influence of his diverse religious background, his guiding principles of church union and the application of these principles in his church work, and his leadership in the World Alliance of Reformed Churches. Basic to Richards' concept of church union was spiritual unity between the churches seeking organic union. Richards was involved in six efforts toward organic union. The only one consummated formed the Evangelical and Reformed Church in 1934.

RICHEY, JAMES ARTHUR MORROW

183. LaFontaine, Charles V. "COBS WITHOUT CORN, WELLS WITHOUT WATER": THE SPIRITUAL ODYSSEY OF JAMES ARTHUR MORROW RICHEY, 1871-1933. *Mid-America 1978 60(2): 107-119.*

James Arthur Morrow Richey was a noted convert from the Protestant Episcopal Church to Roman Catholicism. The son of an Episcopal clergyman, Richey was also educated for that ministry. After serving several parishes he became convinced that he could no longer stay in the Episcopal ministry, and in 1910 he was baptised as a Catholic. From then on he was active in the Catholic Church, being employed often as a journalist.

RICHMAN, JULIA

184. Berrol, Selma. WHEN UPTOWN MET DOWNTOWN: JULIA RICHMAN'S WORK IN THE JEWISH COMMUNITY OF NEW YORK, 1880-1912. *Am. Jewish Hist. 1980 70(1): 35-51.*

Julia Richman (1855-1912) was the first Jewish woman school principal, the first Jewish district superintendent of schools, a founder of the Young Women's Hebrew Association and the National Council of Jewish Women, a director of the Hebrew Free School Association and the Educational Alliance, and a lecturer and author for the Jewish Chautauqua Society. As a Progressive reformer, Richman sought to improve secular and Jewish education to achieve a more orderly, ethical, and equitable society. She criticized East European Jewish immigrants as deficient in moral values, and was in turn criticized by them, yet she continued to work on their behalf. Her career illuminates the Progressive Era, the place of women reformers in it, and the relationship between "uptown" and "downtown" in New York City's Jewish community.

RIGDON, SIDNEY

185. Gregory, Thomas J. SIDNEY RIGDON: POST NAUVOO. *Brigham Young U. Studies 1981 21(1): 51-67.*

Describes the life of Sidney Rigdon (1793-1876), Mormon leader, after he was excommunicated by the Mormons in 1844. Arriving in Pittsburgh, Pennsylvania, he established the Church of Christ. After a short sojourn in Antrim Township, Pennsylvania, he moved in 1847 to Jackson Hill, New York. In late 1850, Rigdon moved into his son-in-law's home in Friendship, New York, living there until early 1859, when he moved into the Friendship home of another son-in-law until his death. In Philadelphia in May 1863 he organized the Church of Jesus Christ of the Children of Zion. Shortly thereafter he asked his counselors and members to move to Attica, Iowa, where they remained until 1875 when they moved near Emerson, Manitoba. His organization was successful during 1864-67 but then declined, dissolving around 1886. Discusses Rigdon's views of Joseph Smith, polygamy, and his relations with other Mormon factions.

186. Rollmann, Hans. THE EARLY BAPTIST CAREER OF SIDNEY RIGDON IN WARREN, OHIO. *Brigham Young U. Studies 1981 21(1): 37-50.*

Traces the Baptist career of Sidney Rigdon (1793-1876), Mormon leader, before he met the Mormons. In 1817 he became a member of the Peter's Creek, Pennsylvania, Baptist Church. He studied for the ministry in North Sewickley, Pennsylvania, in 1818. By 1819 he had been ordained by the Pennsylvania Regular Baptists. In March 1820 Rigdon arrived in Warren, Ohio, and affiliated with the Baptist Church there, marrying Phebe Brook in June. Discusses the formation of the Mahoning Association resulting from a division of the Beaver Baptist Association which would be the forerunner of Alexander Campbell's Disciples of Christ. Rigdon left Warren in early 1822 for a Pittsburgh pastorate.

RIGGS, THOMAS LAWRASON

187. Janick, Herbert. CATHOLICISM AND CULTURE: THE AMERICAN EXPERIENCE OF THOMAS LAWRASON RIGGS, 1888-1943. *Catholic Hist. Rev. 1982 68(3): 451-468.*

The career of Thomas Lawrason Riggs, as the first Roman Catholic chaplain at Yale University from 1922 to 1943, as a patron of *Commonweal* magazine, and as a pioneer in the

National Conference of Christians and Jews, stands in contrast to the stereotype of the American Catholic Church as an immigrant, working-class organization whose members struggled for economic and political power while sealing themselves off from an alien Protestant culture. Riggs is significant because he was an intellectual and a devout Catholic priest. This essay details the way in which he integrated the secular and the spiritual in his own life, and then attempted to guide Catholics into the mainstream of American culture.

RINGGOLD, SAMUEL

188. Ashdown, Paul G. SAMUEL RINGGOLD: A MISSIONARY IN THE TENNESSEE VALLEY, 1860-1911. *Tennessee Hist. Q. 1979 38(2): 204-213.*

Samuel Ringgold (1825-1911) arrived in Bowling Green, Kentucky, as an Episcopal deacon in 1861, just in time to be caught in the middle of a loyalty controversy between the Confederate Episcopal Church and Union troops. Ringgold kept Christ Church (in Bowling Green) neutral and later kept wartime politics out of his church in Knoxville. There Ringgold later became the foremost churchman in eastern Tennessee.

ROBERTS, BRIGHAM HENRY

189. Smith, George D. "IS THERE ANY WAY TO ESCAPE THESE DIFFICULTIES?" THE BOOK OF MORMON STUDIES OF B. H. ROBERTS. *Dialogue 1984 17(2): 94-111.*

Brigham Henry Roberts (1857-1933) devoted his life to studying the *Book of Mormon* . He was rare among the General Authorities of the Church of Jesus Christ of Latter-Day Saints in his willingness to confront conflicts between *Book of Mormon* histories of Native Americans and archaeology, contradictions within the *Book of Mormon* itself, and similarities between legends current in the popular culture of Joseph Smith's social environment and the contents of the *Book of Mormon. His Book of Mormon Difficulties* (1921) and *A Book of Mormon Study* (1923), although often ignored by Mormons, continued to challenge the Mormon Church to duplicate Roberts's own high level of intellectual integrity and scientific rigor.

ROBINSON, FRANK BRUCE

190. Peterson, Keith. FRANK BRUCE ROBINSON AND PSYCHIANA.
Idaho Yesterdays 1979 23(3): 9-15, 26-29.

Frank Bruce Robinson established the world's largest mail-order religion in the 1930's. Operating out of several buildings in Moscow (Idaho), Psychiana was a blend of ideas from the New Thought movement, the beliefs of the power of positive thinking, and the possibility of material success and happiness. Psychiana had appeal to a great many people; they enrolled in correspondence courses to learn more of Robinson's teachings. Covers 1929-48.

ROBINSON, STUART

191. Weeks, Louis. STUART ROBINSON: KENTUCKY PRESBYTERIAN LEADER.
Filson Club Hist. Q. 1980 54(4): 360-377.

Stuart Robinson was minister of the Second Presbyterian Church of Louisville, Kentucky, from 1858 until his death in 1881. Born in Ireland in 1814, Robinson was educated at Amherst and Union Theological Seminary in Virginia. After short pastorates in Kentucky and Maryland, Robinson taught at Danville Seminary between 1856 and 1858. There he wrote the first of three theology texts. After he assumed the Louisville position, he became involved in Civil War controversies and spent most of the war in voluntary exile in Canada. During Reconstruction Robinson was the most active leader in the movement to ally Kentucky Old School Prsbyterians with the southern branch of the church.

ROOSEVELT, FRANKLIN D.

192. Bolt, Robert. FRANKLIN DELANO ROOSEVELT, SENIOR WARDEN, ST. JAMES CHURCH AT HYDE PARK, NEW YORK.
Historical Magazine of the Protestant Episcopal Church 1985 54(1): 91-99.

Describes Franklin D. Roosevelt's role as senior warden of the St. James Episcopal Church, Hyde Park, New York, during his tenure as president. Although president, he took his position in the church in which he had been baptized seriously. As a teenager, Roosevelt had been greatly influenced by Groton School headmaster Endicott Peabody. Endicott criticized "faith divorced from deeds," and this contributed to Roosevelt's belief in responsibility to his church. Numerous incidents reveal a very religious side to the president.

ROOT, OREN

193. Winship, Win. OREN ROOT, DARWINISM AND BIBLICAL CRITICISM.
J. of Presbyterian Hist. 1984 62(2): 111-123.

The new European scientific knowledge came to America during the life of Oren Root. As an educated and informed clergyman of the late 1800's, he faced Darwinism with the unshakable convictions that truth was one and all truths were reconcilable. He thus had little difficulty in adapting evolution to God's special creation. He was not overwhelmed by scientific findings that might or might not coincide with religious belief, believing apparent contradictions to be due to the limitations of the human mind. Regarding biblical criticism, he took a similar track: reverence for the Bible and for scholarship, but not scholarship to the detriment of faith.

ROWEN, MARGARET W.

194. White, Larry. MARGARET W. ROWEN: PROPHETESS OF REFORM AND DOOM.
Adventist Heritage 1979 6(1): 28-40.

Adventist Margaret W. Rowen, who claimed that she had divinely inspired visions, the first on 22 June 1916, and who attempted to prove her divine inspiration in the face of charges by the General Conference and the Southern California Conference of Seventh-Day Adventists by forging documents to prove that she was the successor to prophetess Ellen White, was eventually charged with and convicted of conspiring to murder Dr. Bert E. Fullmer in 1927, even though Fullmer was not murdered.

S

SCHLATTER, FRANCIS

195. Szasz, Ferenc M. FRANCIS SCHLATTER: THE
HEALER OF THE SOUTHWEST.
New Mexico Hist. Rev. 1979 54(2): 89-104.

Francis Schlatter (1856-97), a poor German shoemaker from
Alsace-Lorraine who emigrated to the United States in 1884,
was a product of the social unrest of the 1890's. Drawing
heavily on New Thought ideas, Schlatter wandered across the
southwest between 1893 and his death in 1897 believing that
God had chosen him to perform great deeds of healing.
Schlatter, who did heal some people, claimed that the end of
time was approaching and said that God would establish a New
Jerusalem in America to be located in Datil, New Mexico.

SCHREIBER, EMANUEL

196. Kramer, William M. and Clar, Reva. EMANUEL
SCHREIBER: LOS ANGELES' FIRST REFORM RABBI,
1885-1889.
*Western States Jewish Hist. Q. 1977 9(4): 354-370; 1977 10(1):
38-55.*

Part I. Emanuel Schreiber left his native Germany in 1881.
After serving synagogues in Mobile (Alabama) and Denver
(Colorado) he was invited to Los Angeles' Congregation B'nai
B'rith in 1885. Some of the traditionalists were offended by
Schreiber's radical-Reform policies but the majority of the
congregation supported him. He was active in community
affairs; most significant was his role in the formation of the
Associated Charities which developed into the present United
Crusade. San Francisco journalist Isidore N. Choynski criticized
Rabbi Schreiber's accumulation of wealth from astute land
speculation. *Part II.* Religious and social activities at
Congregation B'nai B'rith were enhanced by the participation of
the rabbi's wife. Reform-Orthodox tensions decreased as Rabbi
Schreiber impressed the Jewish community with his
considerable knowledge of religious phenomena. Schreiber's
relations with the gentile community were excellent; Christian

ministers appreciated his learning and invited him to speak to their congregations. Despite his esteemed position in Los Angeles, Schreiber's ambitions caused him to leave. He served at synagogues in Arkansas, Washington, Ohio, and Illinois, 1889-99. He was minister to Chicago's Congregation Emanu-El from 1899 to 1906 when he moved to the east coast. In 1920 he returned to Los Angeles, where he remained until his death in 1932.

SEYBERT, HENRY

197. Frazier, Arthur H. HENRY SEYBERT AND THE CENTENNIAL CLOCK AND BELL AT INDEPENDENCE HALL.
Pennsylvania Mag. of Hist. and Biog. 1978 102(1): 40-58.

Following his admired father's death, Henry Seybert almost gave up mineralogy, to which he had significantly contributed, and turned to spiritualism. He wandered for 20 years. After 1846 he became involved in Philadelphia civic affairs. The clock and bell, first projected as a public project in 1860, were personally consummated in 1876. Believing he could obtain heaven by helping the poor, he broadly bequeathed his benificence, including the founding of Seybert Institute.

SHANLEY, JOHN

198. Duchschere, Kevin A. JOHN SHANLEY: NORTH DAKOTA'S FIRST CATHOLIC BISHOP.
North Dakota Hist. 1979 46(2): 4-13.

John Shanley, a New York-born priest of Irish descent, became the first Catholic bishop of North Dakota in January 1890, for Jamestown, North Dakota. His earlier clerical career had been mainly spent in St. Paul, Minnesota, where he championed the cause of his black and Italian parishioners and exhibited a pronounced Irish ethnicity and affinity for other ethnics. Throughout his career, Bishop Shanley was an ardent advocate of temperance. In North Dakota the bishop proved to be an indefatigable worker in uniting his far-flung coreligionists through the erection of a network of churches and schools. He displayed considerable sympathy for Indians. He was instrumental in bringing an end to North Dakota's law allowing a 90-day residency for people seeking divorce.

SHIELDS, THOMAS TODHUNTER

199. Russell, C. Allyn. THOMAS TODHUNTER SHIELDS, CANADIAN FUNDAMENTALIST. *Ontario Hist. (Canada) 1978 70(4): 263-280.*

Shields's influence came from his prominence as an evangelical Protestant leader, writer, and speaker. He was born in England in 1873, came to Canada in 1888, and began his ministry in 1891. He was appointed to the Jarvis Street Baptist Church, Toronto, in 1910, and remained there until his death in 1955. The major events of his career, the sources and extent of his influence as a Fundamentalist, and significant controversies are described. Some of the basic points of his theology are also given.

SHIPLEY, JONATHAN

200. King, Irving H. DR. JONATHAN SHIPLEY, DEFENDER OF THE COLONIES, 1773-1775. *Hist. Mag. of the Protestant Episcopal Church 1976 45(1): 25-30.*

Jonathan Shipley (1714-78) was Anglican Bishop of St. Asaph. He was acquainted with the American colonies through his connection with the Society for the Propagation of the Gospel in Foreign Parts. In 1773 he preached a sermon in London before the Society in which he urged Great Britain to rule the colonies justly. In 1774 he published a speech which was supposed to have been given before the House of Lords. In it he strongly opposed the Stamp Act, the Townshend Duties, and the Tea Act. He also urged Parliament not to alter the charter of Massachusetts Bay that year, but to permit the colonists to continue to enjoy the liberty which the English fathers had given them. He was ignored in every instance. Throughout the war Shipley opposed the English effort.

SMITH, ALBERT EDWARD

201. Petryshyn, Jaroslav. FROM CLERGYMAN TO
COMMUNIST: THE RADICALIZATION OF ALBERT
EDWARD SMITH.
J. of Can. Studies (Canada) 1978-79 13(4): 61-71.

After 32 years (1893-1924) as a Methodist pastor in western
Canada, influenced by the Social Gospel, Smith passed through
a Toronto People's Church to the Communist Party. By 1921, he
regarded Christ as a communist thinker and teacher. His
experience as a member of the Manitoba legislature (1921-23)
had convinced him that a Labour Party required discipline and
well-defined objectives. These he found among Communist
Party members.

SMITH, GERALD L. K.

202. Jeansonne, Glen. PREACHER, POPULIST,
PROPAGANDIST: THE EARLY CAREER OF GERALD L.
K. SMITH.
Biography 1979 2(4): 303-327.

Gerald L. K. Smith, born and reared in Wisconsin and educated
in Indiana, served as a Christian minister before becoming Huey
P. Long's Share Our Wealth Society organizer in 1934.
Protestant Fundamentalism and political populism and
progressivism prepared Smith for political activism. His
evolution from radicalism to reaction is examined and the
apparent disjunction explained.

SMITH, HENRY BOYNTON

203. Muller, Richard A. HENRY BOYNTON SMITH:
CHRISTOCENTRIC THEOLOGIAN.
J. of Presbyterian Hist. 1983 61(4): 429-444.

Henry Boynton Smith of New York's Union Theological
Seminary, a New-School Presbyterian, argued in favor of
reunion with Old-School Presbyterians, placing emphasis on the
centrality of Christology in Reformed theology. Rather than
attack errors, Smith attempted to understand them and to build
theology in dialogue rather than defend an established position.

Smith's theological position on the centrality of Christ in the Reformed system contributed greatly to the internal reconciliation of contemporary Presbyterianism, and was in no small measure responsible for the reunion of 1869.

SMITH, JOSEPH

204. Hill, Marvin S. A NOTE ON JOSEPH SMITH'S FIRST VISION AND ITS IMPORT IN THE SHAPING OF EARLY MORMONISM.
Dialogue 1979 12(1): 90-99.

Reviews the religious background of the young Joseph Smith (1805-44) and his family to determine the degree of influence this might have had on the questions he asked (which of the existing Christian religions was the true faith; whether, indeed, there was a Supreme Being). Methodism, Presbyterianism, Universalism, and the thoughts of Thomas Paine and Thomas Jefferson all played a role in Smith's questions about and attitudes toward religion as well as in the doctrines of the Mormon Church which Smith soon founded. As a reflection of Smith's early religious experiences and questions, there remains an uneasy tension between faith and reason in Mormonism to this day.

SMITH, MICHAEL

205. Killingsworth, Myrth Jimmie. THE REVEREND MICHAEL SMITH'S CONTRIBUTION TO COLONIAL LITERARY HISTORY.
Hist. Mag. of the Protestant Episcopal Church 1981 50(4): 369-376.

Between 1752 and 1762 Michael Smith was an Anglican missionary in North Carolina under the auspices of the Society for the Propagation of the Gospel (SPG). His writings reflect that experience. His lengthy poem, *Christianity Unmasqued,* is a commentary on the SPG's endeavors and failures in America. Few poems emerge from the colonial experience in North Carolina, and thus his contribution to Anglo-American literary history is unique as a contribution to religious history. While his published sermons are traditional, his poetry demonstrates a versatile writer able to draw on the secular tradition of 18th-century satire in a bold and original way to give new power to standard Anglican doctrines.

SMITH, WILLIAM B.

206. Edwards, Paul M. WILLIAM B. SMITH: THE PERSISTENT "PRETENDER." *Dialogue 1985 18(2): 128-139.*

William B. Smith was the brother of the Mormon Prophet Joseph Smith and therefore also the uncle of the prophet's son, Joseph Smith III, first president and patriarch of the Reorganized Church of Jesus Christ of Latter Day Saints. Following the 1844 martyrdom of the prophet and his brother Hyrum Smith, William B. Smith was acknowledged as patriarch by the Church of Jesus Christ of Latter-Day Saints. Excommunicated in 1845 by other church leaders who regarded him as a challenge to their authority, he became associated in turn with numerous religious sects. Breaking away from the Mormon mainstream, he even served as a Baptist preacher in New York until charged with heresy. From 1879, he was accepted by the reorganized Mormon Church under his nephew, but as long as he lived there was controversy over his status in the church.

SMITH, WILLIAM (1811-93)

207. Bates, Irene M. WILLIAM SMITH, 1811-93: PROBLEMATIC PATRIARCH. *Dialogue 1983 16(2): 11-23.*

William Smith was the younger brother of the Mormon prophet Joseph Smith. He was rejected as patriarch and apostle by the 6 October 1845 General Conference of the Church of Jesus Christ of Latter-Day Saints. Seeks a more realistic and positive Mormon evaluation of the man, whose conflict with church authorities arose from his feeling that leadership of the restored church should have remained within the prophet's family. He joined the Reorganized Church of Jesus Christ of Latter Day Saints in 1878.

SMOLNIKAR, ANDREAS BERNARDUS

208. Alexander, Jon and Williams, David. ANDREAS
BERNARDUS SMOLNIKAR: AMERICAN CATHOLIC
APOSTATE AND MILLENNIAL PROPHET.
Am. Benedictine Rev. 1984 35(1): 50-63.

Andreas Bernardus Smolnikar was ordained a priest in 1819 in
Yugoslavia and joined the Benedictines in 1825 in Austria. He
came to Boston, Massachusetts, in 1837 and spent the remainder
of his life attempting to convince clerics and laity of a millennial
new era of peace. He neither established a community nor
founded a new denomination. Smolnikar symbolizes the
romantic spirit of antebellum America; his aspirations were vast,
but his accomplishments were ephemeral.

SNOW, ELIZA ROXEY

209. Beecher, Maureen Ursenbach. THE ELIZA ENIGMA.
Dialogue 1978 11(1): 30-43.

Examines the role of Eliza Roxey Snow (1804-87), plural wife
of Joseph Smith and later Brigham Young, in the Mormon
Church. Her poetry, begun in her Ohio youth, was important as
an expression of her faith but undistinguished as poetry. She
spoke in tongues, and was recognized as a prophet by her
contemporaries, but most revelations were derivative, and
predictions half-fulfilled. She practiced priestly functions in
ministering to women in the early church in Utah. Her skills as
"presidentess" were those of a succesful administrator rather
than an originator.

210. Mulvay, Jill C. ELIZA R. SNOW AND THE WOMAN
QUESTION.
Brigham Young U. Studies 1976 16(2): 250-264.

Examines the role of Eliza Roxey Snow in originating and
leading all female Latter-day Saint organizations. As wife of
both Joseph Smith and Brigham Young consecutively, Mrs.
Snow was in a position to help define the status of women
within Mormon society. Comparisons are drawn between the
woman's movement among the Mormons and the other feminist
crusades stirring in America at the same time. Attention is given
to Mrs. Snow's views on women's suffrage, female relief

societies, business and medical efforts by Church women, and female attitudes toward polygamy.

SOLOMON, MICHAEL G.

211. Kramer, William M. and Clar, Reva. MICHAEL G. SOLOMON (1868-1927): RABBI AND LAWYER OF LOS ANGELES.
Western States Jewish Hist. Q. 1981 14(1): 3-29.

Rabbi Michael G. Solomon served Los Angeles's Congregation B'nai B'rith, now Wilshire Boulevard Temple, from 1895 to 1899. Disagreements developed between Solomon and some members of the congregation, particularly over his insistence on equal privileges and standards for all the children in the religious school. Solomon declined to stand for reelection in 1899. He became a practicing attorney in 1903, but alternated this career with temporary employments as rabbi to congregations in distant states. Although he was welcome to stay at all of his positions, for reasons of his own he returned to California.

SPALDING, FRANKLIN SPENCER

212. Sillito, John and Bradley, Martha. FRANKLIN SPENCER SPALDING: AN EPISCOPAL OBSERVER OF MORMONISM.
Historical Magazine of the Protestant Episcopal Church 1985 54(4): 339-349.

Franklin Spencer Spalding was Episcopal Bishop of Utah during 1905-14. He was a careful observer of the Mormon church and the subtle changes that were taking place within Mormonism at the turn of the century. Many of these changes were not recognized by Mormons themselves who believed that the church never evolved. The effort of observers like Spalding is an important legacy for those scholars today, both Mormon and non-Mormon, who are striving to understand more fully Mormon theology, the development of Mormonism as a distinct religious tradition, and its place in American life.

SPIVAK, CHARLES

213. Abrams, Jeanne. CHASING AN ELUSIVE DREAM: CHARLES SPIVAK AND THE JEWISH AGRICULTURAL SETTLEMENT MOVEMENT. *Western States Jewish History 1986 18(3): 204-217.*

Dr. Charles Spivak (1861-1927), "guiding genius" of the Jewish Consumptives' Relief Society, maintained a lifelong interest in Jewish agricultural settlement. He headed the Am Olam group in his home town of Kremenschug, Russia, taught at Alliance Colony in New Jersey, played an active role in the Jewish Alliance of America, collected data on the Atwood and Catopaxi colonies in Colorado, and encouraged agricultural activity at the Jewish Consumptives' Relief Society Hospital, which he directed. Spivak was a maverick both in terms of his communal activities and in terms of his Judaism.

STEFFENS, LINCOLN

214. Shapiro, Herbert. LINCOLN STEFFENS AND THE MCNAMARA CASE: A PROGRESSIVE RESPONSE TO CLASS CONFLICT. *Am. J. of Economics and Sociol. 1980 39(4): 397-412.*

Lincoln Steffens's involvement with the McNamara case (which in 1911 exchanged a commitment to seek labor-capital understanding for prison terms for the two McNamara brothers in the *Los Angeles Times* building dynamiting) was one of the major concerns of his life. His *Autobiography* is not fully dependable regarding this incident; churches were not uniformly hostile to the settlement that ended the case and the *Los Angeles Times,* ignoring commitments to meet labor grievances, maintained its antiunion position. Steffens's experimentation with "Golden Rule" Christian love as an alternative to class conflict reflected his divergent allegiances to corporate capitalism. It also reflected his own rejection of class partisanship. Although the pledges made in the settlement were broken, Steffens remained loyal to the McNamaras and continued to argue it is futile to punish individuals for acts rooted in social conflict.

STONE, EDWIN MARTIN

215. Lovett, Robert W. THE DUAL CAREERS OF REV. EDWIN M. STONE. *Essex Inst. Hist. Collections 1983 119(2): 81-94.*

Edwin Martin Stone (1804-1883), Unitarian minister of the Second Church of Beverly during 1833-47, wrote a *History of Beverly* (1843), which remains the most complete account of the town. Includes biographical sketch of Stone, tracing early years, ministerial career, and activities as state representative. His "assiduous labors in digging up and preserving the raw materials of history are still of benefit to scholars who came after him." Even when he left Beverly for a ministry-at-large in Providence, Rhode Island, in 1847, he still remained active as a historian by writing on Rhode Island history.

STONE, ELLEN M.

216. Woods, Randall B. TERRORISM IN THE AGE OF ROOSEVELT: THE MISS STONE AFFAIR, 1901-1902. *Am. Q. 1979 31(4): 478-495.*

In September 1901, Ellen M. Stone (1846-1927), an American Congregationalist missionary, was kidnapped and held for ransom by a group of Macedonian nationalists called the Internal Macedonian Revolutionary Organization. During her captivity, the Roosevelt administration, the American public, and Stone's organization, the American Board Commissioners for Foreign Missions, struggled with the issues of international political terrorism. A $66,000 ransom raised by public donations was ultimately accepted by the nationalists, who then freed Stone in February 1902. The ransom helped finance a Macedonian rebellion in August 1903 that was quickly suppressed by the Turks.

STONEBERG, PHILIP J.

217. Ijams, Ethel W. PHILIP J. STONEBERG AND THE PRESERVATION OF BISHOP HILL. *Swedish-American Historical Quarterly 1985 36(1): 26-38.*

Bishop Hill, Illinois, a religious communistic settlement founded by Eric Janson and his Swedish followers, flourished during 1846-61 and is now being preserved as a National Historic Landmark. Philip J. (christened Jonas Philip) Stoneberg (1875-1919) was the grandson of colonists Jonas and Anna Stoneberg. Although he received degrees from Knox College and Columbia and Harvard universities, he spent his career in Bishop Hill as an educator and local historian. He collected documents, reminiscences, and oral histories of the settlement, wrote papers on its history, and delivered historical orations at pioneer celebrations.

STRANG, JAMES JESSE

218. Lewis, David Rich. "FOR LIFE, THE RESURRECTION, AND THE LIFE EVERLASTING": JAMES J. STRANG AND STRANGITE MORMON POLYGAMY, 1849-1856. *Wisconsin Mag. of Hist. 1983 66(4): 274-291.*

James Jesse Strang led a schismatic faction out of the Mormon Church and established a "Garden of Peace" at Voree in southeastern Wisconsin. In 1847 he moved his community to Beaver Island in northern Michigan, and there openly espoused his views on polygamy. Although previously opposed to the practice, he eventually took five wives.

STRONG, JOSIAH

219. Muller, Dorothea R. CHURCH BUILDING AND COMMUNITY MAKING ON THE FRONTIER, A CASE STUDY: JOSIAH STRONG, HOME MISSIONARY IN CHEYENNE, 1871-1873. *Western Hist. Q. 1979 10(2): 191-216.*

Congregationalist minister Josiah Strong (b. 1847) served his first pastorate as a home missionary in Cheyenne, Wyoming, 1871-73. The two years' experience shaped his religious perspective and influenced the development of society and institutions of Cheyenne—its community-making process. Strong's enthusiastic commitment to evangelize the nation and indirectly the world was developed here. He proclaimed a buoyant nationalism in a widely influential volume in the

1880's, and for three decades he led national organizations that espoused his Social Gospel message and perpetuated his dream of America's world-evangelizing role.

STUART, OSCAR J. E.

220. Forness, Norman O. THE MASTER, THE SLAVE, AND THE PATENT LAWS: A VIGNETTE OF THE 1850S. *Prologue 1980 12(1): 23-28.*

Oscar J. E. Stuart, a lawyer in Pike City, Mississippi, tried to get a patent on an invention created by his slave Ned. According to Stuart, the master owned the manual and intellectual fruits of his slave's labor and this satisfied the requirement of the law that patents only be issued to persons who could swear that the inventions were products of their own genius. The patent application was submitted to Commissioner of Patents Joseph Holt. The merits of the application were judged against the patent legislation of 4 July 1836, and Attorney General Jeremiah S. Black denied the patent application for "a double cotton scraper." Undaunted in his efforts, Stuart proceeded to manufacture cotton scrapers in Mississippi and published a broadside offering them for sale.

SWEET, H. C.

221. Kydd, Ronald. H. C. SWEET: CANADIAN CHURCHMAN. *J. of the Can. Church Hist. Soc. (Canada) 1978 20(1-2): 19-30.*

In many ways Dr. H. C. Sweet demonstrated his unique character. First, as missionary, minister, and professor, he served several Christian denominations. Second, he was well-educated and maintained his intellectual curiosity all his life; he obtained the doctorate in theology at the age of 61. Third, he carried out his Christian commitment in a variety of ways. In his early years he was a missionary to Indians in Saskatchewan. Later he served as pastor to a black congregation in Winnipeg. He also devoted a number of years to Christian education through his teaching at two theological institutions. Beloved and respected, H. C. Sweet had such diversity in his career that he merits special attention among Canadian clergy.

SWEET, WILLIAM WARREN

222. Ash, James L., Jr. AMERICAN RELIGION AND THE ACADEMY IN THE EARLY TWENTIETH CENTURY: THE CHICAGO YEARS OF WILLIAM WARREN SWEET. *Church Hist. 1981 50(4): 450-464.*

William Warren Sweet, professor of American Christianity at the Divinity Schools of the University of Chicago, was an influential figure in the modern academic study of religion. Sweet, who was educated at Ohio Wesleyan University and Drew Theological Seminary, had studied American History at the University of Pennsylvania. He adopted scientific historiographical methods to the American Protestantism experience on the frontier. During his 19 years on the Chicago faculty, Sweet oversaw the dissertations of future church history scholars Sidney Mead, Robert Handy, and Winthrop Hudson.

SWENSSON, CARL AARON

223. Pearson, Daniel M. THE TWO WORLDS OF CARL A. SWENSSON, 1873-1888. *Swedish Pioneer Hist. Q. 1977 28(4): 259-273.*

Carl Aaron Swensson was the founder of Bethany College, Lindsborg, Kansas. Several biographical sketches have been written since his death in 1904 but few have analyzed his life and his importance, both in American society and in Midwest Swedish immigrant communities. Swensson's father, Jonas, was a Lutheran minister who despised many aspects of American culture, so he did not allow his children to attend public schools or find American friends. Thus Carl grew up a Swede. He attended Augustana College and Seminary during 1873-79 which further enhanced his Swedish orientation. But he realized that the promise of America was not only that it was Christian, but that it was energetic, strong, and educated. After he graduated, he added Swedish immigrant colonization projects, politics, and railroad promotion to his active concern for religious education. Describes his efforts in these areas.

SYLVESTER, JAMES JOSEPH

224. Feuer, Lewis S. AMERICA'S FIRST JEWISH PROFESSOR: JAMES JOSEPH SYLVESTER AT THE UNIVERSITY OF VIRGINIA. *American Jewish Archives 1984 36(2): 152-201.*

Describes James Joseph Sylvester's academic career at the University of Virginia, where he was welcomed in 1841 as one of the foremost mathematicians of his time. Soon after his arrival, however, his appointment was criticized because he was Jewish. Student Robert Lewis Dabney incited others to threaten Sylvester, and he eventually left the university. Before Johns Hopkins University hired Sylvester as professor of mathematics in 1876, his departure from the University of Virginia was reexamined and Sylvester was found to be blameless. The university's records, however, suggest that attempts were made to suppress any suggestion of guilt on the part of the students who attacked Sylvester, and it is clear that Sylvester's departure in 1842 was a forced resignation. Sylvester held various teaching positions and eventually reclaimed his stature as the preeminent mathematician of his time.

SYSOEV, IVAN

225. Kolesnikoff, James D. and Kolesnikoff, Nina. IVAN SYSOEV: A DOUKHOBOR POET. *Can. Ethnic Studies (Canada) 1980 12(1): 93-102.*

Ivan Sysoev (1894-1967), a self-taught Doukhobor poet, began writing verses at age 14. His early lyrics, short landscape sketches, reproduce impressions from nature. In many respects Sysoev's early verses resemble Koltsov's poetry in admiration for nature, simplicity of language, and melody. Beginning with the 1920's, the poet addresses the theme of Doukhobor history and ideals. With pride he writes about his forefathers who in 1895 burned their arms and refused to do military service. He portrays them as true Christian martyrs. The poet considers "thou shall not kill" the most important tenet of Doukhobor philosophy, and skillfully uses poetic imagery to proclaim pacifist ideas. His mature poetry relies on simple and concrete images which frequently refer to visible objects or scenes. With concrete and realistic objects Sysoev creates highly spiritual poetry. Not only does concretizing poetic images not contradict the deep religious direction of the poetry, but this technique actually enhances it.

T

TALMAGE, JAMES E.

226. Rowley, Dennis. INNER DIALOGUE: JAMES TALMAGE'S CHOICE OF SCIENCE AS A CAREER, 1876-84.
Dialogue 1984 17(2): 112-130.

English Mormon immigrant James E. Talmage arrived in Utah in 1876 at age 14. For eight years he attended Brigham Young Academy, where the teaching, example, and encouragement of its principal, Karl G. Maeser, brought out in the young man a strong desire to study natural science, which Maeser reconciled with Mormon religious doctrines. As early as 1879, Talmage began teaching science courses at the academy, supplementing his training there by subsidized extramural tutoring from local chemists. In 1882, he reluctantly moved "to the infidel and anti-Mormon east" to study the sciences extensively at Lehigh College in South Bethlehem, Pennsylvania, and at Johns Hopkins in Baltimore. His laboratory studies frequently consisted of catching and killing small animals to examine their internal organs. He returned to Utah in 1884, fully prepared for a career in science.

TALMAGE, THOMAS DEWITT

227. Szasz, Ferenc M. T. DEWITT TALMAGE: SPIRITUAL TYCOON OF THE GILDED AGE.
J. of Presbyterian Hist. 1981 59(1): 18-32.

Although one of the most powerful and influential pulpit masters of his day, the influence of Presbyterian Thomas DeWitt Talmage (1832-1902) hardly extended beyond his own generation. The issues and qualities which reflected his greatness do not appeal to the modern mind. His enormous success lay in his dramatic reinforcement of older views and simultaneous soothing of fears about the new. Among his major themes were labor/capital difficulties, the higher criticism of the Bible, and the theory of evolution. Even when criticizing society Talmage used Victorian rather than scriptural standards. Because he had little doctrine to support his position, he helped dilute the Protestant tradition. This weakened US Protestantism's efforts to confront the dilemmas of the 20th century.

TANNER, JERALD AND SANDRA

228. Foster, Lawrence. CAREER APOSTATES: REFLECTIONS ON THE WORKS OF JERALD AND SANDRA TANNER. *Dialogue 1984 17(2): 35-60.*

Jerald and Sandra Tanner left the Church of Jesus Christ of Latter-Day Saints in 1959 to become fundamentalist Protestants. They then devoted their lives to trying to destroy the Mormon community by publishing caustic and telling criticisms of Mormon history and practice. Although church authorities and even Mormon historians avoided confronting the Tanners, many of the issues they raised were of concern also to Mormon historians, who, however, approached them without anti-Mormon bias or hysteria. In a paradoxical way, the Tanners themselves exemplify many of the strengths and weaknesses of the Mormon tradition.

TAYLOR, JOHN

229. Kristjanson, Wilhelm. JOHN TAYLOR AND THE PIONEER ICELANDIC SETTLEMENT IN MANITOBA AND HIS PLEA ON BEHALF OF THE PERSECUTED JEWISH PEOPLE. *Tr. of the Hist. and Sci. Soc. of Manitoba (Canada) 1975-76 32: 33-41.*

Some Icelanders had settled in Utah by 1855, but large-scale emigration to North America began in the 1870's. Originally settling in Ontario, many followed missionary John Taylor (1812-84) to colonize in Manitoba. While suffering hardships, the colony survived and welcomed immigrants until World War I, with a peak of 1,700 in 1887. Also, reacting to an outbreak of anti-Jewish persecution in Czarist Russia in the 1880's, Taylor urged that the refugees be officially invited to colonize the Canadian frontier, repeating the Icelanders' experience.

TAYLOR, WILLIAM

230. Turner, Charles W. "CALIFORNIA" TAYLOR OF ROCKBRIDGE: "BISHOP TO THE WORLD." *Southern California Q. 1980 62(3): 229-238.*

William Taylor (1821-1902), Methodist bishop from Rockbridge County, Virginia, was a prominent preacher whose missionary work took him to three continents. Taylor came to California in 1849 and preached to San Francisco's gamblers and miners. He worked in California for seven years, founding churches, supporting reforms in mental health facilities, and calling for schools and protective reservations for Indians. He is credited with supplying the Australian Eucalyptus seeds that started the species on the west coast. He founded and supported missions in Asia, Latin America, and Africa, and in 1884 was designated Bishop of Africa. His last years were spent in retirement in California.

THOBURN, ISABELLA

231. Brown, Earl Kent. ISABELLA THOBURN. *Methodist History 1984 22(4): 207-220.*

Isabella Thoburn went as a missionary to India in 1870 under the sponsorship of the Women's Home Missionary Society of the Methodist Church. There she established schools for Indian girls and women, the central subject being English. While on furlough to the United States, she became a proponent for Indian female education, founded a training school for deaconesses, and served as administrator of a hospital in Cincinnati. Upon returning to India she founded the Lucknow Woman's College (now Isabella Thoburn College).

THORNTON, THOMAS C.

232. Rogers, Tommy W. T. C. THORNTON: A METHODIST EDUCATOR OF ANTEBELLUM MISSISSIPPI.
J. of Mississippi Hist. 1982 44(2): 136-146.

Born in 1794 in Dumfries, Virginia, Thomas C. Thornton moved to Mississippi in 1841 after his appointment to the presidency of Centenary College at Brandon Springs. From 1841 until his death in 1860, Thornton continued as a pivotal figure in the development of denominational education in the state. The author sketches Thornton's affiliation with Centenary College, the College of Jackson, Brandon College, and Madison College, and traces the successes and failures experienced by these institutions under Thornton's direction. Also included is Senator Albert Gallatin Brown's praise of Thornton's defense of slavery entitled, *An Inquiry Into Slavery.* Brown's expression of appreciation for this Southern educator, who served as the "paragon of Methodist influence on behalf of higher education in antebellum Mississippi," may well have served as his eulogy.

TITSWORTH, JUDSON

233. Derge, John. IN SEARCH OF THE KINGDOM IN MILWAUKEE: JUDSON TITSWORTH AND THE SOCIAL GOSPEL: 1883-1909.
Mid-America 1984 66(3): 99-109.

Describes the views and activities of Social Gospel advocate and Congregationalist clergyman Judson Titsworth while he was minister at Plymouth Church in Milwaukee during 1883-1909. Titsworth was a friend of labor, a promoter of church programs for the lower classes, and he hoped to see the new immigrants assimilated into mainstream society. He succeeded more as a publicist of his vision than as an implementer of it.

TOLLES, FREDERICK BARNES

234. Hench, John B. OBITUARY: FREDERICK BARNES TOLLES.
Pro. of the Am. Antiquarian Soc. 1975 85(2): 367-369.

A remembrance of Frederick Barnes Tolles (1915-75). Tolles was born in New Hampshire. He was educated at Harvard University, where he converted from Unitarianism to Quakerism, a decision that was to alter his entire life. He began teaching at Swarthmore College, a Quaker institution, and refused induction in World War II as a conscientious objector, doing alternative work instead. His primary academic thrust was in the direction of the history of Quakerism in the American society and he published a number of books on the subject. Tolles was elected to membership in the American Antiquarian Society in 1967. He was proud of the honor, but distance and poor health prevented him from taking an active part in the Society's activities.

TOWNSEND, CHARLES COLLINS

235. Fisher, Marcelia C. THE ORPHAN'S FRIEND:
CHARLES COLLINS TOWNSEND AND THE ORPHANS'
HOME OF INDUSTRY.
Palimpsest 1979 60(6): 184-196.

The Reverend Charles Collins Townsend (1808-69) was an Episcopalian missionary and the organizer of The Orphans' Home of Industry in Iowa City, Iowa, 1854-68; it housed 500 children from New York City's streets and slums, until the Johnson County Board of Supervisors asked the City Attorney to enjoin the Home from bringing any more orphans to town.

V

VAN DIEREN, JOHANN BERNHARD

236. Jacobsen, Douglas. JOHANN BERNHARD VAN
DIEREN: PEASANT PREACHER AT HACKENSACK, NEW
JERSEY, 1724-40.
New Jersey History 1982 100(3-4): 14-29.

Johann Bernhard Van Dieren, an itinerant minister, eventually settled in Hackensack, New Jersey, in 1725 after several failures at securing a pastorate elsewhere. Not educated formally or even ordained by any denomination, Van Dieren felt himself capable of leading either a Lutheran or Reformed congregation; he finally wound up with a Lutheran one. His credentials were challenged by Lutheran Church officials and in 1733 Van Dieren vacated the parsonage in which he lived. He was popular with his rural congregants, however, because they thought of him as one of their own. He was able to understand and relate to their peasant-like way of life.

VERNER, SAMUEL PHILLIPS

237. Crawford, John R. PIONEER AFRICAN MISSIONARY: SAMUEL PHILLIPS VERNER. *J. of Presbyterian Hist. 1982 60(1): 42-57.*

Samuel Phillips Verner was a Southern Presbyterian missionary to the Belgian Congo. His brief but stormy missionary career, 1895-98, influenced him profoundly and enabled him to rise momentarily close to the creative activity and power toward which he yearned. Verner viewed Africa in general, the Congo in particular, as standing at historical crossroads, and he desired the Anglo-Saxon influence to be the dominating factor. But it was his inability to work within the guidelines of the Foreign Missions Board of the Presbyterian Church in the United States that kept him in constant hot water. Thus when he became seriously ill the board relieved him of his labors. Yet he accomplished a great deal in his brief tenure: he explored parts of the Kasai District, brought back to the Smithsonian numerous ethnological, geological, and zoological specimens, urged the church to concentrate on converting the young Congolese, and forwarded the use of the Tshiluba tongue for Presbyterian work in the Congo.

VIDAVER, HENRY

238. Margolies, Morris B. THE AMERICAN CAREER OF RABBI HENRY VIDAVER. *Western States Jewish Hist. 1983 16(1): 28-43.*

Traces the American career of Henry Vidaver, an immigrant Polish Jew, who arrived in America in 1859 and served as rabbi of congregations in Philadelphia, St. Louis, New York, and San Francisco. Vidaver's career reflected tensions that prevailed in American Jewish communities of the late 19th century.

VINCENT, JOHN HEYL

239. Stephens, Bruce M. MAIL ORDER SEMINARY: BISHOP JOHN HEYL VINCENT AND THE CHAUTAUQUA SCHOOL OF THEOLOGY. *Methodist Hist. 1976 14(4): 252-295.*

John Heyl Vincent (1832-1920), Methodist preacher and bishop, was very conscious of his own lack of education. To assist fellow ministers who also lacked education, he established the degree-granting Chautauqua School of Theology in New York in 1881 to provide correspondence courses and summer sessions. By 1898 the school dropped the granting of degrees and Vincent's dream of theological education for hundreds of untrained Protestant clergymen was short-lived.

VINCENT, THOMAS

240. Snyder, Marsha. THOMAS VINCENT, THE ARCHDEACON OF MOOSONEE. *Ontario Hist. (Canada) 1976 68(2): 119-135.*

Presents a biography of Archdeacon Thomas Vincent and attempts to assess his work for the Anglican Church and the Church Missionary Society in northern Canada. Vincent was born in the North and returned there after his education in the South. He was involved in missionary work before his ordination and thereafter made it his career. Discusses the relationship between the Church Missionary Society and the Hudson's Bay Company, and comments on the impact of Vincent's efforts during his 50 years of service. Remarks on his relationships with colleagues and others, and shows that some of the problems he faced derived, in part, from his intense evangelicism.

VOORSANGER, JACOB

241. Zwerin, Kenneth C. and Stern, Norton B. JACOB VOORSANGER: FROM CANTOR TO RABBI. *Western States Jewish Hist. Q. 1983 15(3): 195-202.*

Jacob Voorsanger (1852-1908), rabbi of San Francisco's Reform Congregation Emanu-El from 1889 until his death, was a self-taught spiritual leader. He lacked formal rabbinical training and ordination; he served his first three congregations as a cantor rather than a rabbi. Because of his impressive scholarly and organizational accomplishments, it was sometimes assumed that he had a university degree and seminary training.

VOTH, HENRY S.

242. Penner, Peter. GUARDIAN OF THE WAY: THE FARMER PREACHER, HENRY S. VOTH (1878-1953). *Mennonite Life 1982 37(3): 8-13.*

The life of Henry S. Voth exemplifies the *reiseprediger* (itinerant farmer-preacher) role in the Mennonite church. Before 1930, Voth lived and preached in Oregon, Minnesota, and Manitoba; during 1930-53, his major role was as a church conference member. His primary method of preaching was to use familiar texts with anecdotes, using the same sermon with varying anecdotes many times. The combination of traveling and preaching with the maintenance of a farm put considerable strain on Voth and his family.

W

WALKER, MARY RICHARDSON

243. Horner, Patricia V. MARY RICHARDSON WALKER: THE SHATTERED DREAM OF A MISSIONARY WOMAN. *Montana 1982 32(3): 20-31.*

Mary Richardson Walker wanted to be a missionary first and a housewife second. She kept a diary during 1833-79 reflecting her personal views of her life and duties at the Tshimakain Indian Mission in eastern Washington and Forest Grove, Oregon. The diaries reveal an intelligent, articulate, and pious woman whose dreams of missionary work were shattered by the tasks and obligations of a pioneer wife.

WARKENTIN, JOHANN

244. Penner, Peter. BY REASON OF STRENGTH: JOHAaNN WARKENTIN, 1859-1948. *Mennonite Life 1978 33(4): 1-9.*

Johann Warkentin (1859-1948), a little-known leader of the Mennonite Brethren Church in Canada, was born in South Russia and migrated to Manitoba in 1879. In 1881 he married Sara Krahn Loewen (d. 1930). Eventually he became a prosperous farmer and they had 19 well-spaced children. Converted from Old Colony Mennonite to Mennonite Brethren, Warkentin served in the Sunday School, directed the choir, and studied theology. Ordained in the Gospel ministry in 1895, he became assistant moderator to the Reverend David Dyck in the Winkler congregation, and moderator in 1906. As part of his missionary outreach interest, he helped establish a MB group in Winnipeg. Warkentin continued active church leadership until 1931 and remained influential for 10 more years.

WATT, GEORGE D.

245. Watt, Ronald G. SAILING "THE OLD SHIP ZION": THE LIFE OF GEORGE D. WATT. *Brigham Young U. Studies 1977 18(1): 48-65.*

George D. Watt (1815-81), the first Mormon convert to be baptized in Great Britain, served as a clerk in Brigham Young's office, as a founding editor of the *Journal of Discourses,* as one of the developers of the Deseret alphabet, and as an early proponent of silkworm culture in Utah. He made significant contributions to the Mormons' cause. His knowledge of stenography particularly aided in the compilation of a written record of the early theological teachings. However, Watt's personality, his questioning of many church doctrines, and his perennial financial straits engendered disputes with many of the Mormon elders and led eventually to his excommunication in 1874.

WATTSON, PAUL

246. LaFontaine, Charles V. FATHER PAUL WATTSON OF GRAYMOOR AND PRAYER FOR CHRISTIAN UNITY. *Catholic Hist. Rev. 1981 67(1): 31-49.*

Reverend Paul Wattson (1863-1940) founder of the Society of the Atonement, began the Church Unity Octave at Graymoor, Garrison, New York, in January 1908. A controversialist in the Protestant Episcopal Church and an advocate of the reunion of Anglicans with the Church of Rome, Father Wattson began the Octave in response to a suggestion by Spencer Jones, an Anglican priest, who shared many of Wattson's views. The Octave was one of several practical expressions of Wattson's conception of the nature of Church unity. After the Society of the Atonement was received into the Roman Catholic Church in 1909, Father Wattson continued to promote the Octave and was able to obtain formal papal approval of the annual observance (January 18-25), although he failed to have it declared universally obligatory. Eventually,Wattson's Octave was broadened in scope and vision by a French Catholic Priest, Paul Irenee Couturier. Today, the observance, begun by Wattson and revised by Couturier, is known as the Week of Prayer for Christian Unity.

WEIGEL, GUSTAVE

247. Collins, Patrick W. GUSTAVE WEIGEL: AN UNCOMPROMISING ECUMENIST. *J. of Ecumenical Studies 1978 15(4): 684-703.*

Gustave Weigel, a Jesuit theologian and educator who died in 1964, was one of the leaders in improving Roman Catholic and Protestant relations since 1950. He defined the Protestant principle as dependence on experience, the intellect, and the Bible. Catholics, on the other hand, depend on magisterial authority more than Protestants. He was an expert on characterizing varieties of Protestantism and became an authority on Protestant theology, particularly that of Paul Tillich. He was active in ecumenical organizations such as Faith and Order, attended the early sessions of Vatican II, and encouraged ecumenical dialogue between students of Woodstock College and Protestant divinity schools.

WELLS, EMMELINE B.

248. Madsen, Carol Cornwall. EMMELINE B. WELLS: "AM I NOT A WOMAN AND A SISTER?" *Brigham Young U. Studies 1982 22(2): 161-178.*

A history of the career of Emmeline Belos (Blanche) Woodward Wells (1828-1921), Mormon editor and suffragette. For 40 years she was active in the women's rights movement. She was active in the Mormon Church Women's Department and was elected general president of the Relief Society in 1910. She also served for 37 years as editor of the Mormon publication, the *Woman's Exponent.* Comments on her 1895 speech to the National-American Woman's Suffrage Association convention. Describes in detail the events in her life leading up to this occasion. Discusses how these spheres of activity interacted and assisted each other. She was not bashful in lecturing on her religious views before an assembly of non-Mormon women. Describes their reaction to her presence and speeches at national suffragist meetings. Although Wells was not unique in her time, it was a unique time in Mormon history.

WILLIAMS, GEORGE WASHINGTON

249. Franklin, John Hope. GEORGE WASHINGTON WILLIAMS: THE MASSACHUSETTS YEARS. *Pro. of the Am. Antiquarian Soc. 1982 92(2): 243-263.*

George Washington Williams (1849-91), born in Pennsylvania, was a soldier, clergyman, editor, lawyer, legislator, historian, diplomat, lecturer, and world traveler. After attending Howard University, Wayland Seminary, and the Newton Theological Institution, he became pastor to the leading Baptist Church in Boston's black community. Fourteen months later he left and traveled widely. Never able to settle down for long in one place, Williams worked for years on *A History of the Negro Race in America from 1619 to 1880* (published in two volumes, 1882-83). Outlines the remainder of Williams's careers and life.

WILLIAMS, ROGER

250. LaFantasie, Glenn W. ROGER WILLIAMS: THE INNER AND OUTER MAN. *Canadian Review of American Studies (Canada) 1985 16(4): 375-394.*

Celebrated historically as a controversialist, advocate of radical ecclesiastical ideas, and peacemaker in colonial New England, Roger Williams asserted that only the inner self revealed a person's spirituality. Consequently, he perceived no incongruity between his fomenting of controversy and his peacemaking. Williams's axiom has since influenced his chroniclers to stress his inner self, to ignore his outer self and, thus, to dismiss Williams's other qualities that also were sources of his greatness.

WILLIAMS, WILLIAM

251. Gura, Philip F. SOWING FOR THE HARVEST: WILLIAM WILLIAMS AND THE GREAT AWAKENING. *J. of Presbyterian Hist. 1978 56(4): 326-341.*

William Williams (1655-1741), uncle of Jonathan Edwards and neighbor of Solomon Stoddard, pastored the church in Hatfield, Massachusetts, from 1686 until his death. While historians of the Great Awakening and of developing Presbyterianism in the Connecticut River Valley know less about Williams than about Edwards or Stoddard, urges that there is enough concerning Williams's career to mark him as significant. Williams's conception of the ministry and his emphasis on the doctrine of the Great Salvation complemented Stoddard's treatises on the nature and necessity of the conversion experience. Williams was not a mere imitation of the more famous Stoddard, but a man of considerable accomplishment and influence in his own right. He believed that the millenium would come in the Valley and that he would have had a part in its consummation.

WINANS, WILLIAM

252. Holder, Ray. PARSON WINANS' PILGRIMAGE TO "THE NATCHEZ," WINTER OF 1810. *J. of Mississippi Hist. 1982 44(1): 47-67.*

William Winans became the leading Methodist minister in Mississippi. Describes his journey to the Natchez area and the beginning of his ministry in the Old Southwest in 1810. Provides information on the area's inhabitants, their religious devotion and practices, and the trials and tribulations faced by Winans in ministering to the Natchez frontier society.

253. Holder, Ray. PARSON WINANS AND MR. CLAY: THE WHIG CONNECTION, 1843-1846. *Louisiana Hist. 1984 25(1): 57-75.*

William Winans, a leading Methodist preacher in Louisiana and Mississippi, worked to prevent the split between northern and southern Methodism. An ardent Whig and personal friend of President William Henry Harrison, he looked to Henry Clay to restore the nation to Whig principles and save the Union. Between 1843 and 1846 Winans and Clay had several personal discussions as well as correspondence on religious and political matters.

WINTHROP, NATHANIEL TAYLOR

254. Chase, Theodore. NATHANIEL TAYLOR WINTHROP. *Massachusetts Hist. Soc. Pro. 1980 92: 163-166.*

Nathaniel Taylor Winthrop, a 10th generation Winthrop and a descendant of Governor John Winthrop, died on 30 June 1980. Winthrop was a kind-hearted man who cherished his family life and devoted much of his energy and wealth to charitable causes. Showing an openness for innovative ideas, he served on such programs as the Experiment in International Living. Winthrop traveled widely in Asia and Africa and took an interest in the socioeconomic plight of the people he encountered. He believed that the study of religion was a key ingredient in promoting international harmony, and for this reason he worked with such groups as the Laymen's Movement for a Christian World and the Council of Religion in International Affairs. His most important contribution to the Massachusetts Historical Society was his ability to locate a collection of 23 original manuscripts, which included letters of the Winthrop family and Roger Williams.

WOLFE, THOMAS

255. Trotti, John Boone. THOMAS WOLFE: THE
PRESBYTERIAN CONNECTION.
J. of Presbyterian Hist. 1981 59(4): 517-542.

Discusses the relationship of the American novelist Thomas
Wolfe (1900-38) and the Presbyterian Church, particularly the
First Presbyterian Church, Asheville, North Carolina, which he
attended until he went away to college. There are numerous
references to this congregation in his autobiographical novel,
Look Homeward, Angel (1929). Although never a communicant
member of the church, he nevertheless felt very close to its life.
Also traces his religious connection through his student days and
later years. The Calvinistic theology he imbibed through
catechetical memorization remained with him and surfaces
throughout his works. His own lifelong posture toward
institutional Christianity was that of the inquirer, the listener, the
critic, mildly amused, yet not fully committed. In a wistful way,
he was attracted to the Christian faith and, in a personal way, to
Presbyterianism.

WRIGHT, HAROLD BELL

256. Jones, Charles T. BROTHER HAL: THE PREACHING
CAREER OF HAROLD BELL WRIGHT.
Missouri Hist. Rev. 1984 78(4): 387-413.

Prints a biography of Harold Bell Wright's years in the ministry.
Although dissatisfied with preaching, Wright had a sensitivity
for the people he encountered in church that helped make him a
popular novelist. Most of his readers were church people whose
concerns and experiences he reflected. Wright grew up in New
York and Ohio, attended Hiram College, and became a minister
in the Christian Church (Disciples of Christ). He worked in
Pennsylvania and the Midwest.

Y

YOUNG, BRIGHAM

257. Coates, Lawrence G. BRIGHAM YOUNG AND MORMON INDIAN POLICIES: THE FORMATIVE PERIOD, 1836-1851.
Brigham Young U. Studies 1978 18(3): 428-452.

Brigham Young's attitudes toward Indians had a profound effect on Mormon-Indian affairs during his lifetime, and even for decades after his death. Traces Young's relationships with Indians from his first mission to them in western New York in 1835, to the exodus from Nauvoo and on the Great Plains, and through his formulation of a policy toward Indians in Utah. Documents Young's evolving socio-religious-humanitarian philosophy. Young was not averse to open conflict with the Indians of Utah when peaceful means failed. He eventually concluded, however, that "it was cheaper to feed the Indians than fight them."

258. Cornwall, Rebecca and Palmer, Richard F. THE RELIGIOUS AND FAMILY BACKGROUND OF BRIGHAM YOUNG.
Brigham Young U. Studies 1978 18(3): 286-310.

Examines the 18th-century religious and family roots of Brigham Young in an effort to determine how that industrious painter and carpenter from western New York came to exercise the leadership of perhaps the "most sensational institutional experiment to come out of the American frontier." The authors search for clues in his heritage, and place Young's New England, Congregational-Methodist forebears within the religious environment of their own age. Young may have been influenced by the mysticism inherent in many of the frontier religions.

259. Jessee, Dean C. BRIGHAM YOUNG'S FAMILY: PART I, 1824-1845.
Brigham Young U. Studies 1978 18(3): 311-327.

Discusses Young as the head of his domestic household, one of the largest families in Mormondom. Many details of Young's private life are sketchy. Assesses Young's personality on the basis of how well he performed his domestic role. The years of instability, 1824-45, cover the period from his first marriage to the family's exodus from Nauvoo. These years were characterized by numerous and extended absences from his family as he served the Mormon Church in America and England.

260. Jessee, Dean C. BRIGHAM YOUNG'S FAMILY: THE WILDERNESS YEARS.
Brigham Young U. Studies 1979 19(4): 474-500.

An account of the trials and tribulations of the family of Brigham Young during the Mormon migration from Nauvoo, Illinois, to Salt Lake City, Utah. Young already had numerous wives; the time, energy, and thought-consuming problems connected with directing the migration while simultaneously establishing a new home in the West left little time for his family. The wives and children did not leave as a unit, and several returned to Nauvoo or went from camp to camp. Their sufferings, faith, and efforts to communicate with their husband are carefully detailed.

261. Moorman, Donald R. SHADOWS OF BRIGHAM YOUNG AS SEEN BY HIS BIOGRAPHERS.
Utah Hist. Q. 1977 45(3): 252-264.

Important biographies of Brigham Young (1801-77), are: Edward W. Tullidge, *Life of Brigham Young,* Morris Robert Werner, *Brigham Young,* Susa Young Gates, *The Life Story of Brigham Young,* Stanley P. Hirshson, *The Lion of the Lord: A Biography of Brigham Young,* and Ray B. West, *Kingdom of the Saints: The Story of Brigham Young and the Mormons.* These representations of sainted father, false prophet, heavenly leader, divine oracle, and unscrupulous financier, do not adequately examine his temperament, Biblicism, and intellectualism.

262. Shipps, Jan. BRIGHAM YOUNG AND HIS TIMES: A CONTINUING FORCE IN MORMONISM.
Journal of the West 1984 23(1): 48-54.

Examines the 30-year career of "Brother Brigham" for reasons why the pioneer-politician-patriach outshone his predecessor, Joseph Smith. Two common assumptions—that the death of

Joseph Smith unified the Saints and that a majority of Mormons left Nauvoo, Illinois, for Utah—are challenged. The trek to the Great Salt Lake Valley and the period during which the Kingdom of Zion was being built up are identified as the opportunities over which Young exercised his extraordinary leadership and established his influence, which persists to the present.

YOUNG, BRIGHAM BICKNELL

263. Cannon, Kenneth L., II. BRIGHAM BICKNELL YOUNG, MUSICAL CHRISTIAN SCIENTIST. *Utah Hist. Q. 1982 50(2): 124-138.*

The life and career of Brigham Bicknell Young, nephew of Mormon leader Brigham Young, began in Salt Lake City. Musically educated in London, England, at the National Training School where he married Eliza Massucato, he taught at Watford School of Music. Acclamation followed as he toured Salt Lake City, New York City, Omaha, and Chicago, where he and his wife converted to Christian Science. The remainder of his life saw his rise in church activities, survival after a schism, leadership, and high esteem as church teacher.

Z

ZUBLY, JOHN JOACHIM

264. Pauley, William E., Jr. TRAGIC HERO: LOYALIST JOHN J. ZUBLY. *J. of Presbyterian Hist. 1976 54(1): 61-81.*

The Swiss-born Reverend John J. Zubly (1724-81), pastor of the Independent Presbyterian Church, Savannah, Georgia, heroically articulated the principles upon which the colonies sought redress of grievances from the crown government. He could not or would not, however, alter his principles to include the possibility of political separation from the mother country. He was an independent thinker who analyzed the Anglo-American relationship in ways that closely paralleled the major voices of patriotic thinking in other colonies, but he arrived at different conclusions concerning the wisdom and justice of seeking political separation. Consistent in his thinking to the end, he died a broken man.

SUBJECT INDEX

Each biographical summary in this book is indexed below with a group (or "string") of index terms. Each of the terms in these strings will move around to the first or leading position in the string so that the entire index string will appear in the subject index as many times as there are terms in the string. This way, there are several different ways to access each biographical summary.

Each of the index strings appears in alphabetical order according to the leading term in bold. If a leading term is exactly the same as the leading term of the string preceding it, then it is replaced by a dash.

The final term in the string is a number in italics; this number refers to the number of the entry, not the page number on which the entry appears. The dates that precede the italicized entry number are the dates of the time period covered by the biographical article.

A

Acculturation. Jewish Theological Seminary. New York City. Theology. 1920's. *109*

Adventists. Fullmer, Bert E. Visions. 1916-29. *194*

Africa. American Colonization Society. Colonization. Medical Education. Presbyterian Church. Slavery. 1840-50. *139*

—. Asia. California. Latin America. Methodist Church. Missions and Missionaries. 1849-1902. *230*

African Methodist Episcopal Church. Blacks. Clergy. College Presidents. Lutheran Church. Wilberforce University. 1830-93. *168*

Agricultural College of Utah, Logan. Brigham Young

College. Colleges and Universities. Educational Administrators. Mormons. State Politics. Utah. 1894-1907. *110*

Agriculture. California (San Fernando Valley). Immigration. Sheep Raising. 1836-82. *116*

—. Judaism. Reform. 1880's-1923. *115*

Alabama. Bishops. Catholic Church. Humor. 1826-54. *173*

—. Child labor movement. Episcopal Church, Protestant. 1890-1907. *153*

Alaska (Cape Prince of Wales). Lopp, W. T. ""Tom". Missions and Missionaries. 1892-1902. *122*

Alaska Herald. Editors. Far Western States. Priests. Ukrainian Americans. 1832-1916. *93*

Alberta (Red Deer River area). Homesteaders. Missionaries. Personal narratives. Saskatchewan. Women. 1905-64. *30*

Allegheny Mountains. Catholic Church. Clergy. Missions and Missionaries. Pennsylvania, western. 1799-1840. *77*

Alline, Henry. New Lights. Nova Scotia. Sects, Religious. 1769-1834. *169*

American Board Commissioners for Foreign Missions. Internal Macedonian Revolutionary Organization. Kidnapping. Macedonia. Missions and Missionaries. Roosevelt, Theodore (administration). Terrorism. 1901-02. *216*

American Colonization Society. Africa. Colonization. Medical Education. Presbyterian Church. Slavery. 1840-50. *139*

American Friend. Editors. Friends, Society of. Pennsylvania. Periodicals. 1893-1912. *108*

American Missionary Association. Blacks. Missions and Missionaries. New York. Reconstruction. South. Teachers. 1865-77. *143*

American Revolution. Antislavery Sentiments.

Congregationalism. Rhode Island (Newport). ca 1770-1803. *95*

—. Calvinists. Clergy. Jefferson, Thomas. 1775-1808. *119*

—. Clergy. Loyalists. Massachusetts (Deerfield). 1766-80. *5*

—. New Jersey. Politics. Religion. 1770-90. *83*

American Revolution (antecedents). Church and state. Connecticut. Politics. Theologians. 1714-71. *59*

—. Church of England. Colonial Government. Great Britain. 1773-75. *200*

—. Friends, Society of. Political Attitudes. 1737-77. *165*

Andover Theological Seminary. Diaries. Hawaii. Middlebury College. Missions and Missionaries. 1815-39. *21*

Anglican Communion. Education. Governors. Patronage. Philanthropy. Societies. 1686-1728. *156*

Antinomianism. Immortality (doctrine). Massachusetts. 1638. *98*

Antislavery Sentiments. American Revolution. Congregationalism. Rhode Island (Newport). ca 1770-1803. *95*

—. Civil War. Friends, Society of. Maine. Military Service. 1850's-64. *107*

—. Clergy. Presbyterian Church, Reformed. Vermont (Ryegate). 1785-1820. *142*

Anti-Zionist sentiment. Colorado (Denver). Jews. Patriotism. 1889-1938. *74*

Apostasy. Mormons. 1959-82. *228*

Apostolic Delegates. Catholic Church. Quebec. 1877-78. *51*

Archivists. California. Franciscans. Historians. Mission Santa Barbara. 1937-77. *280*

Art criticism. California. Catholic Church. Missions and Missionaries. 1769-1980. *157*

Asia. Africa. California. Latin America. Methodist Church. Missions and Missionaries. 1849-1902. *230*

Assimilation. Georgia (Atlanta). Jews. Rabbis. 1903-70. *78*

—. Indians (agencies). Presbyterian Church. 1870-82. *123*

—. Jews. Zionism. 1914-40's. *148*

Attitudes. Bermuda. Blacks. Canada. Church of England. Feild, Edward. Race Relations. 1825-50. *100*

Authors. Christianity. Indians, Mohegan. Missionaries. 1760's-92. *160*

—. Clergy. Disciples of Christ. Midwest. Pennsylvania. 1896-1908. *256*

Autobiography. Clergy. Daily Life. Delaware (Sussex County). Methodist Protestant Church. 1780-1857. *146*

—. Clergy. Methodists. 1810's-50's. *41*

Avery, Martha Moore. Catholic Truth Guild. Evangelists. 1917-41. *81*

B

Baptist Historical Society. Louisiana. Publishers and Publishing. 1850-1900. *86*

Baptists. Blacks. Clergy. Massachusetts (Boston). 1870's-91. *249*

—. Clergy. Louisiana (northern). Social Conditions. 1860-96. *85*

—. Conservatism. First Baptist Church (Fort Worth). Politics. Texas. 1900-50. *159*

—. Fundamentalism. Ontario (Toronto). 1891-1955. *199*

—. Great Britain. Massachusetts (Middleborough). New England. Theology. 1745-65. *6*

—. Language. Micmac Indians. Missions and Missionaries. Nova Scotia. 1830-89. *176*

—. Missions and Missionaries. Oklahoma (Wichita Mountains). Women's American Baptist Home Missionary Society. 1893-1961. *54*

—. Ohio (Warren). 1817-22.
186

Baptists (American). China.
Siam. 1865-90. *72*

Baptists, Southern. Ecumenism.
ca 1890-1928. *151*

Beaconites. Bible. Crewdson,
Isaac. Great Britain. Quakers.
Schisms. 1833-37. *13*

Belgian Congo. Missions and
Missionaries. Presbyterian
Church (Southern). 1895-98.
237

Benedictines. Catholic Church.
Millenarianism. 1837-69. *208*

Bereavement. Children. Death
and Dying. ca 1700. *130*

Bermuda. Attitudes. Blacks.
Canada. Church of England.
Feild, Edward. Race Relations.
1825-50. *100*

Bethel Ships. Evangelism.
Merchant Marine. Methodist
Church. New York City.
Swedish Americans. 1832-66.
17

Bible. Beaconites. Crewdson,
Isaac. Great Britain. Quakers.
Schisms. 1833-37. *213*

Biography. Mormons. 1943-78.
112

Bishops. Alabama. Catholic
Church. Humor. 1826-54.
173

—. Canada. Church of England.
Hudson's Bay Company.
Missionaries. Rupert's Land.
1839-85. *3*

—. Church of Ireland. Irish
Canadians. Ontario. 1861-
1901. *118*

—. Episcopal Church, Protestant.
Mormons. Social Change.
Utah. 1905-14. *212*

—. Methodism. Missions and
Missionaries. Philippines.
Singapore. 1854-1937. *161*

Black Hills. Episcopal Church,
Protestant. Missionaries.
1860-76. *92*

Blacks. African Methodist
Episcopal Church. Clergy.
College Presidents. Lutheran
Church. Wilberforce
University. 1830-93. *168*

—. American Missionary
Association. Missions and
Missionaries. New York.
Reconstruction. South.
Teachers. 1865-77. *143*

—. Attitudes. Bermuda.
Canada. Church of England.
Feild, Edward. Race Relations.
1825-50. *100*

—. Baptists. Clergy.
Massachusetts (Boston).
1870's-91. *249*

—. Church of England. Georgia.
Missions and Missionaries.
Political Leadership. Silk
industry. 1735-75. *164*

—. Clergy. 1831-41. *61*

—. Clergy. Methodist Episcopal
Church, African. New York
City. 1787-1875. *60*

—. Clergy. Social Gospel.
Socialism. 1880's-90's. *177*

—. Georgia (Valdosta). Religious Leaders. 1899-1914. *8*

—. Indian-White Relations. 17c-1792. *15*

—. Presbyterian Church. South. 1930-75. *26*

Book of Mormon. Exegesis. Mormons. Theology. 1823-1984. *189*

Brattle Street Church. Elites. Gentility (concept). Massachusetts (Boston). Puritans. 1715-45. *49*

Brigham Young College. Agricultural College of Utah, Logan. Colleges and Universities. Educational Administrators. Mormons. State Politics. Utah. 1894-1907. *110*

C_____

California. Africa. Asia. Latin America. Methodist Church. Missions and Missionaries. 1849-1902. *230*

—. Archivists. Franciscans. Historians. Mission Santa Barbara. 1937-77. *80*

—. Art criticism. Catholic Church. Missions and Missionaries. 1769-1980. *157*

—. Catholic Church. Mission Santa Barbara. Missionaries. Southwestern history. 1851-1934. *70*

—. Franciscans. Historians. Mission Santa Barbara. 1901-77. *79*

—. Jews. Newspapers. Publishers. Rabbis. San Francisco *Voice of Israel.* San Francisco *Weekly Gleaner.* 1854-61. *19*

California (Los Angeles). Judaism (Reform). 1881-1932. *196*

—. Judaism (Reform). Lawyers. Rabbis. Wilshire Boulevard Temple. 1895-1927. *211*

California (San Bernardino). Charities. Henrietta Hebrew Benevolent Society. Jews. Women. 1870-91. *2*

California (San Fernando Valley). Agriculture. Immigration. Sheep Raising. 1836-82. *116*

California (San Francisco). Chinese Americans. Missions and Missionaries. Presbyterian Mission Home. Women. 1869-1920. *38*

—. Jews. Missouri (St. Louis). New York City. Pennsylvania (Philadelphia). Rabbis. 1859-82. *238*

—. Judaism. 1857-69. *89*

—. Judaism (Reform). Rabbis. 1873-1908. *241*

Calvinism. First Presbyterian Church of Topeka. Kansas. Psychology. 1930-80. *141*

—. Trinitarians. Unitarianism. 1780-1840. *45*

Calvinistic Methodist Church. Missionaries. Nebraska, eastern. 1853-60. *57*

Calvinists. American Revolution. Clergy. Jefferson, Thomas. 1775-1808. *119*

—. Revivals. Theologians. 1719-1850. *132*

Canada. Attitudes. Bermuda. Blacks. Church of England. Feild, Edward. Race Relations. 1825-50. *100*

—. Bishops. Church of England. Hudson's Bay Company. Missionaries. Rupert's Land. 1839-85. *3*

—. Catholic Church. Clergy. Illinois, central. Illinois (Kankakee area). Immigrants. Presbyterian Church. 1830-99. *46*

—. Clergy. Educators. Statesmen. 1902-35. *162*

—. Clergy. Methodists. 1880-86. *24*

—. Communist Party. Labour Party. Methodism. Social Gospel. 1893-1924. *201*

—. Dukhobors. Poetry. 1909-67. *225*

—. Evangelism. Holiness Movement Church. Methodist Church. 1887-1921. *96*

—. Irish Americans. Kentucky (Louisville). Leadership. Presbyterian Church. 1858-81. *191*

—. Protestantism. 1866-1960. *221*

Canada, western. Church of England. Hudson's Bay

Company. Missionaries. 1844-64. *97*

Canon law. Circumcision. Europe. Judaism (Orthodox). Louisiana (New Orleans). 1853-65. *99*

Cape Verde Islands. Missions and Missionaries. North Carolina. Poetry. 1752-62. *205*

Cardinals. Catholic Church. Illinois (Chicago). 20c. *152*

Catholic Church. 1888-1943. *187*

—. Alabama. Bishops. Humor. 1826-54. *173*

—. Allegheny Mountains. Clergy. Missions and Missionaries. Pennsylvania, western. 1799-1840. *77*

—. Apostolic Delegates. Quebec. 1877-78. *51*

—. Art criticism. California. Missions and Missionaries. 1769-1980. *157*

—. Benedictines. Millenarianism. 1837-69. *208*

—. California. Mission Santa Barbara. Missionaries. Southwestern history. 1851-1934. *70*

—. Canada. Clergy. Illinois, central. Illinois (Kankakee area). Immigrants. Presbyterian Church. 1830-99. *46*

—. Cardinals. Illinois (Chicago). 20c. *152*

—. Chaplains. Confederate Army. 10th Confederate Infantry. 1851-64. *25*

—. Church of England. Clergy. Maryland. 1774-97. *27*

—. Church Unity Octave. Ecumenists. Episcopal Church, Protestant. Society of the Atonement. 1908-40. *246*

—. Clergy. Converts. Episcopal Church, Protestant. ca 1900-33. *183*

—. Clergy. Letters. Pennsylvania (Pittsburgh). 1885-1921. *39*

—. Clergy. Polish Americans. 1863-1913. *114*

—. Ecumenism. Protestantism. 1950-64. *247*

—. Educators. Minnesota. Sisters of St. Joseph of Corondelet. 1842-1930. *101*

—. Episcopal Church, Protestant. Rites and Ceremonies. Vermont. 1832-68. *94*

—. Fenians. Ireland. Pennsylvania (Philadelphia). Speeches, Addresses, etc. Wood, James F. 1839-75. *149*

—. Franciscan Sisters. Minnesota (Winona). St. Teresa, College of. Women. 1903-54. *145*

—. Irish Americans. Minnesota (St. Paul). North Dakota (Jamestown Diocese). 1852-1909. *198*

—. Sioux Indians. South Dakota. Yankton Reservation (Marty Mission). 1918-49. *66*

—. Supreme Court Justices. 19c-20c. *35*

Catholic Truth Guild. Avery, Martha Moore. Evangelists. 1917-41. *81*

Centennial Celebrations. Civic affairs. Independence Hall. Pennsylvania (Philadelphia). Philanthropy. 1793-1882. *197*

Chaplains. Catholic Church. Confederate Army. 10th Confederate Infantry. 1851-64. *25*

—. Presbyterians. Scholars. Teachers. 1770's-1809. *137*

Chaplains, Army. Civil War. Episcopal Church, Protestant. South or Southern States. 1851-72. *10*

Charities. California (San Bernardino). Henrietta Hebrew Benevolent Society. Jews. Women. 1870-91. *2*

—. Mormon Relief Society (Social Services Department). Utah. 1919-29. *125*

Charity of Providence, Sisters of. Construction. Pacific Northwest. Pioneers. 1856-1902. *129*

Chautauqua School of Theology. Methodist Church. New York. Seminaries, correspondence. 1881-98. *239*

Chicago, University of (Divinity School). Colleges and Universities. Illinois.

Religious historians. 1927-46.
222

Child labor movement.
Alabama. Episcopal Church,
Protestant. 1890-1907. *153*

Children. Bereavement. Death
and Dying. ca 1700. *130*

China. Baptists (American).
Siam. 1865-90. *72*

Chinese Americans. California
(San Francisco). Missions and
Missionaries. Presbyterian
Mission Home. Women.
1869-1920. *38*

Christian Catholic Church.
Evangelism. Illinois (Zion).
1888-1907. *62*

Christian Science. ca 1840-
1910. *65*

—. Educators. Musicians. 1856-
1938. *263*

—. Personality. Shakers.
Theology. 1736-1910. *64*

Christianity. Authors. Indians,
Mohegan. Missionaries.
1760's-92. *160*

—. Class Struggle. *Los Angeles
Times*. McNamara case.
Progressivism. Radicals and
Radicalism. 1908-12. *214*

Church administrators. New
York (Hyde Park). Presidents.
St. James Episcopal Church.
1933-45. *192*

Church and state. American
Revolution (antecedents).
Connecticut. Politics.
Theologians. 1714-71. *59*

—. Church of England
(opposition to). Presbyterian
Church. ca 1750-90. *121*

—. Supreme Court. 1949-67. *47*

Church of Christ. Church of
Jesus Christ of the Children of
Zion. Mormons. 1844-76.
185

Church of England. American
Revolution (antecedents).
Colonial Government. Great
Britain. 1773-75. *200*

—. Attitudes. Bermuda. Blacks.
Canada. Feild, Edward. Race
Relations. 1825-50. *100*

—. Bishops. Canada. Hudson's
Bay Company. Missionaries.
Rupert's Land. 1839-85. *3*

—. Blacks. Georgia. Missions
and Missionaries. Political
Leadership. Silk industry.
1735-75. *164*

—. Canada, western. Hudson's
Bay Company. Missionaries.
1844-64. *97*

—. Catholic Church. Clergy.
Maryland. 1774-97. *27*

—. Clergy. Connecticut.
Heretics. 1720-82. *14*

—. Clergy. Maryland. ca 1745-
68. *7*

—. Clergy. Virginia. 1743-52.
58

—. Congregationalism.
Massachusetts. 1720-30. *56*

—. Hudson's Bay Company.
Manitoba (Red River
Settlement). Missionaries.
1823-38. *106*

—. Missions and Missionaries. Ontario (Moosonee). 1835-1910. *240*

Church of England (opposition to). Church and State. Presbyterian Church. ca 1750-90. *121*

Church of Ireland. Bishops. Irish Canadians. Ontario. 1861-1901. *118*

Church of Jesus Christ of the Children of Zion. Church of Christ. Mormons. 1844-76. *185*

Church Unity Octave. Catholic Church. Ecumenists. Episcopal Church, Protestant. Society of the Atonement. 1908-40. *246*

Circumcision. Canon law. Europe. Judaism (Orthodox). Louisiana (New Orleans). 1853-65. *99*

Civic affairs. Centennial Celebrations. Independence Hall. Pennsylvania (Philadelphia). Philanthropy. 1793-1882. *197*

Civil Rights Activists. Clergy. Education. ca 1934-55. *113*

Civil War. Antislavery Sentiments. Friends, Society of. Maine. Military Service. 1850's-64. *107*

—. Chaplains, Army. Episcopal Church, Protestant. South or Southern States. 1851-72. *10*

—. Deacons. Episcopalians. Kentucky (Bowling Green).

Tennessee (Knoxville). 1860-1911. *188*

—. Episcopal Church, Protestant. Reconstruction. Theology. 1860-1914. *63*

—. Publishers and Publishing. Reconstruction. State Politics. Tennessee. Unionists. 1825-77. *32*

Class Struggle. Christianity. *Los Angeles Times.* McNamara case. Progressivism. Radicals and Radicalism. 1908-12. *214*

Clergy. African Methodist Episcopal Church. Blacks. College Presidents. Lutheran Church. Wilberforce University. 1830-93. *168*

—. Allegheny Mountains. Catholic Church. Missions and Missionaries. Pennsylvania, western. 1799-1840. *77*

—. American Revolution. Calvinists. Jefferson, Thomas. 1775-1808. *119*

—. American Revolution. Loyalists. Massachusetts (Deerfield). 1766-80. *5*

—. Antislavery Sentiments. Presbyterian Church, Reformed. Vermont (Ryegate). 1785-1820. *142*

—. Authors. Disciples of Christ. Midwest. Pennsylvania. 1896-1908. *256*

—. Autobiography. Daily Life. Delaware (Sussex County). Methodist Protestant Church. 1780-1857. *146*

—. Autobiography. Methodists. 1810's-50's. *41*

—. Baptists. Blacks. Massachusetts (Boston). 1870's-91. *249*

—. Baptists. Louisiana (northern). Social Conditions. 1860-96. *85*

—. Blacks. 1831-41. *61*

—. Blacks. Methodist Episcopal Church, African. New York City. 1787-1875. *60*

—. Blacks. Social Gospel. Socialism. 1880's-90's. *177*

—. Canada. Catholic Church. Illinois, central. Illinois (Kankakee area). Immigrants. Presbyterian Church. 1830-99. *46*

—. Canada. Educators. Statesmen. 1902-35. *162*

—. Canada. Methodists. 1880-86. *24*

—. Catholic Church. Church of England. Maryland. 1774-97. *27*

—. Catholic Church. Converts. Episcopal Church, Protestant. ca 1900-33. *183*

—. Catholic Church. Letters. Pennsylvania (Pittsburgh). 1885-1921. *39*

—. Catholic Church. Polish Americans. 1863-1913. *114*

—. Church of England. Connecticut. Heretics. 1720-82. *14*

—. Church of England. Maryland. ca 1745-68. *7*

—. Church of England. Virginia. 1743-52. *58*

—. Civil Rights Activists. Education. ca 1934-55. *113*

—. Colorado (Conejos). Daily life. Jesuits. Letters. 1874-80. *9*

—. Composers. Gospel music. Methodist Church. 1890's-1958. *16*

—. Edwards, Jonathan. Evangelism. Great Awakening. Missions and Missionaries. 1742-1850's. *28*

—. Farmers. Manitoba. Mennonite Brethren Church. Russian Canadians. 1879-1948. *244*

—. First Presbyterian Church. Social Reform. Washington (Seattle). 1880's-1920. *135*

—. Franciscans. Polish Americans. 1824-91. *144*

—. Historians. Massachusetts (Beverly). Rhode Island. Unitarianism. 1833-47. *215*

—. Immigrants. Merchants. Presbyterians. Quebec (Montreal). Scottish Canadians. 1824-75. *133*

—. Liberals. Missouri (St. Louis). Protestants. Universalists. 1867-1923. *43*

—. Loyalists. Presbyterian Church. 1770-81. *264*

—. Lutheran Church. New Jersey (Hackensack). 1724-40. *236*

—. Manitoba. Mennonites. Minnesota. Oregon. 1900-53. *242*

—. Massachusetts (Northampton). Puritans. Sermons. Stoddard, Solomon. 1658-69. *131*

—. Missionaries. Nova Scotia (Lunenburg). St. John's Anglican Church. 1814-25. *1*

—. Montana. Presbyterian Church. Sunday schools. Travel. 1870's-1927. *68*

—. Mormons. 1830-45. *207*

—. Mormons. 1833-93. *206*

—. Mormons. Theology. 1834-73. *124*

—. Protestantism. 1895-1950. *155*

—. Religious Education. 1775. *84*

—. Science. Theology. 1866-1900. *193*

College Presidents. African Methodist Episcopal Church. Blacks. Clergy. Lutheran Church. Wilberforce University. 1830-93. *168*

College Teachers. Discrimination. Jews. Johns Hopkins University. Virginia, University of. 1841-77. *224*

Colleges and Universities. Agricultural College of Utah, Logan. Brigham Young College. Educational

Administrators. Mormons. State Politics. Utah. 1894-1907. *110*

—. Chicago, University of (Divinity School). Illinois. Religious historians. 1927-46. *222*

Colonial Government. American Revolution (antecedents). Church of England. Great Britain. 1773-75. *200*

Colonization. Africa. American Colonization Society. Medical Education. Presbyterian Church. Slavery. 1840-50. *139*

—. Icelandic Canadians. Jews. Manitoba. Refugees. Russia. 1870-90. *229*

Colorado (Conejos). Clergy. Daily life. Jesuits. Letters. 1874-80. *9*

Colorado (Denver). Anti-Zionist sentiment. Jews. Patriotism. 1889-1938. *74*

Colorado, northeastern. Frontier and Pioneer Life. Methodist Episcopal Church (North, South). Women. 1874-91. *175*

Communist Party. Canada. Labour Party. Methodism. Social Gospel. 1893-1924. *201*

Composers. Clergy. Gospel music. Methodist Church. 1890's-1958. *16*

Confederate Army. Catholic Church. Chaplains. 10th

Confederate Infantry. 1851-64. *25*

Conference on Jewish Relations. Jews. Philosophy. Values. 1880-1947. *48*

Conflict. Peace. Philosophy. 1630-84. *250*

Congregational Church. Missionaries. South Dakota (Oahe). 1875-1910. *50*

Congregationalism. American Revolution. Antislavery Sentiments. Rhode Island (Newport). ca 1770-1803. *95*

—. Church of England. Massachusetts. 1720-30. *56*

—. Converts. Family. Missions and Missionaries. Vermont. 1789-1819. *20*

—. Family. Methodism. Mormons. New England. New York, western. 18c-1830's. *258*

—. Missions and Missionaries. Nationalism. Social Gospel. Wyoming (Cheyenne). 1871-1916. *219*

Congregationalists. Plymouth Church. Social Gospel. Wisconsin (Milwaukee). 1880-1915. *233*

Connecticut. American Revolution (antecedents). Church and state. Politics. Theologians. 1714-71. *59*

—. Church of England. Clergy. Heretics. 1720-82. *14*

Connecticut Valley. Great Awakening. Massachusetts

(Hatfield). Presbyterian Church. 1686-1741. *251*

Conservatism. Baptists. First Baptist Church (Fort Worth). Politics. Texas. 1900-50. *159*

—. Jews. Philosophy. Sociology. 1927-77. *90*

Construction. Charity of Providence, Sisters of. Pacific Northwest. Pioneers. 1856-1902. *129*

Converts. Catholic Church. Clergy. Episcopal Church, Protestant. ca 1900-33. *183*

—. Congregationalism. Family. Missions and Missionaries. Vermont. 1789-1819. *20*

—. Mormons. Negroes. Slavery. Utah (Salt Lake City). 1844-76. *44*

Correspondence courses. Idaho (Moscow). Psychiana (religion). 1929-48. *190*

Cotton scrapers. Inventions. Mississippi. Patent laws. Slavery. ca 1850. *220*

Courtship. Great Britain (London). Indians, Ojibway. Jones, Peter. Methodism. New York. 1820's-33. *71*

Crewdson, Isaac. Beaconites. Bible. Great Britain. Quakers. Schisms. 1833-37. *13*

D

Daily Life. Autobiography. Clergy. Delaware (Sussex County). Methodist Protestant Church. 1780-1857. *146*

—. Clergy. Colorado (Conejos). Jesuits. Letters. 1874-80. *9*

—. Letters. Missionaries. Oregon. 1840-80. *178*

Darwinism. Episcopal Church, Protestant. Europe. Excommunications. Hermeneutics. Ohio (Canton). St. Paul's Church. 1890-91. *127*

Deacons. Civil War. Episcopalians. Kentucky (Bowling Green). Tennessee (Knoxville). 1860-1911. *188*

Death and Dying. Bereavement. Children. ca 1700. *130*

Delaware (Sussex). Diaries. 1839-57. *147*

Delaware (Sussex County). Autobiography. Clergy. Daily Life. Methodist Protestant Church. 1780-1857. *146*

Diaries. Andover Theological Seminary. Hawaii. Middlebury College. Missions and Missionaries. 1815-39. *21*

—. Delaware (Sussex). 1839-57. *147*

—. Frontier and Pioneer Life. Missions and Missionaries. Oregon (Forest Grove). Tshimakain Indian Mission. Washington. 1833-97. *243*

—. Kentucky. Missions and Missionaries. North Central States. Presbyterian Church. 1828-45. *180*

—. Minnesota, northern. Missionaries. Wisconsin. 1833-49. *69*

Disciples of Christ. Authors. Clergy. Midwest. Pennsylvania. 1896-1908. *256*

Discrimination. College Teachers. Jews. Johns Hopkins University. Virginia, University of. 1841-77. *224*

Documents. Missions and Missionaries. Western States. 1850-72. *120*

Dukhobors. Canada. Poetry. 1909-67. *225*

E

Ecumenism. Baptists, Southern. ca 1890-1928. *151*

—. Catholic Church. Protestantism. 1950-64. *247*

—. Evangelical and Reformed Church. Presbyterian Church. World Alliance of Reformed Churches. 1900-55. *182*

—. Presbyterian Church, New School. Slavery issue. 1840's. *52*

Ecumenists. Catholic Church. Church Unity Octave. Episcopal Church, Protestant. Society of the Atonement. 1908-40. *246*

Editors. *Alaska Herald.* Far Western States. Priests. Ukrainian Americans. 1832-1916. *93*

—. *American Friend.* Friends, Society of. Pennsylvania. Periodicals. 1893-1912. *108*

Editors and Editing. Temperance Movements.

Tennessee. *Whig* (newspaper). 1838-51. *31*

Education. Anglican Communion. Governors. Patronage. Philanthropy. Societies. 1686-1728. *156*

—. Civil Rights Activists. Clergy. ca 1934-55. *113*

—. Mormons. Science. 1876-84. *226*

Educational Administrators. Agricultural College of Utah, Logan. Brigham Young College. Colleges and Universities. Mormons. State Politics. Utah. 1894-1907. *110*

Educational Reformers. Jews. New York City. Social Reformers. Women. 1880-1912. *184*

Educators. Canada. Clergy. Statesmen. 1902-35. *162*

—. Catholic Church. Minnesota. Sisters of St. Joseph of Corondelet. 1842-1930. *101*

—. Christian Science. Musicians. 1856-1938. *263*

—. Immigrants. Midwest. Swedish Americans. 1873-1904. *223*

—. India. Methodist Church. Missionaries. Women. Women's Home Missionary Society. 1865-1901. *231*

Edwards, Jonathan. Clergy. Evangelism. Great Awakening. Missions and Missionaries. 1742-1850's. *28*

Edwards, Jonathan. *(Account of the Life of the Late Reverend Mr. David Brainerd)*. Evangelism. 1739-1842. *29*

Elites. Brattle Street Church. Gentility (concept). Massachusetts (Boston). Puritans. 1715-45. *49*

Episcopal Church, Protestant. Alabama. Child labor movement. 1890-1907. *153*

—. Bishops. Mormons. Social Change. Utah. 1905-14. *212*

—. Black Hills. Missionaries. 1860-76. *92*

—. Catholic Church. Church Unity Octave. Ecumenists. Society of the Atonement. 1908-40. *246*

—. Catholic Church. Clergy. Converts. ca 1900-33. *183*

—. Catholic Church. Rites and Ceremonies. Vermont. 1832-68. *94*

—. Chaplains, Army. Civil War. South or Southern States. 1851-72. *10*

—. Civil War. Reconstruction. Theology. 1860-1914. *63*

—. Darwinism. Europe. Excommunications. Hermeneutics. Ohio (Canton). St. Paul's Church. 1890-91. *127*

—. Groton School. Massachusetts. 1884-1940. *170*

—. Heresy. New York (Rochester). Reform. St.

Andrew's Church. Trials. 1879-1927. *53*

—. Iowa (Iowa City). New York City. Orphans' Home of Industry. 1854-68. *235*

Episcopalians. Civil War. Deacons. Kentucky (Bowling Green). Tennessee (Knoxville). 1860-1911. *188*

Europe. Canon law. Circumcision. Judaism (Orthodox). Louisiana (New Orleans). 1853-65. *99*

—. Darwinism. Episcopal Church, Protestant. Excommunications. Hermeneutics. Ohio (Canton). St. Paul's Church. 1890-91. *127*

Evangelical and Reformed Church. Ecumenism. Presbyterian Church. World Alliance of Reformed Churches. 1900-55. *182*

Evangelism. Bethel Ships. Merchant Marine. Methodist Church. New York City. Swedish Americans. 1832-66. *17*

—. Canada. Holiness Movement Church. Methodist Church. 1887-1921. *96*

—. Christian Catholic Church. Illinois (Zion). 1888 1907. *62*

—. Clergy. Edwards, Jonathan. Great Awakening. Missions and Missionaries. 1742-1850's. *28*

—. Edwards, Jonathan *(Account of the Life of the Late Reverend*

Mr. David Brainerd). 1739-1842. *29*

—. Religious Education. 1807-52. *163*

Evangelists. Avery, Martha Moore. Catholic Truth Guild. 1917-41. *81*

Excommunications. Darwinism. Episcopal Church, Protestant. Europe. Hermeneutics. Ohio (Canton). St. Paul's Church. 1890-91. *127*

Exegesis. *Book of Mormon.* Mormons. Theology. 1823-1984. *189*

F_____

Faith healing. New Thought. Southwest. 1893-97. *195*

Family. Congregationalism. Converts. Missions and Missionaries. Vermont. 1789-1819. *20*

—. Congregationalism. Methodism. Mormons. New England. New York, western. 18c-1830's. *258*

—. Illinois (Nauvoo). Mormons. New York. 1824-45. *259*

Far Western States. *Alaska Herald.* Editors. Priests. Ukrainian Americans. 1832-1916. *93*

Farmers. Clergy. Manitoba. Mennonite Brethren Church. Russian Canadians. 1879-1948. *244*

—. Jews. Settlement. 1861-1927. *213*

Feild, Edward. Attitudes. Bermuda. Blacks. Canada. Church of England. Race Relations. 1825-50. *100*

Feminism. Friends, Society of. Social Reform. ca 1820-80. *150*

Fenians. Catholic Church. Ireland. Pennsylvania (Philadelphia). Speeches, Addresses, etc. Wood, James F. 1839-75. *149*

Fiction. Louisiana (New Orleans). Presbyterian Church. ca 1870-1925. *37*

First Baptist Church (Fort Worth). Baptists. Conservatism. Politics. Texas. 1900-50. *159*

First Presbyterian Church. Clergy. Social Reform. Washington (Seattle). 1880's-1920. *135*

First Presbyterian Church of Topeka. Calvinism. Kansas. Psychology. 1930-80. *141*

Franciscan Sisters. Catholic Church. Minnesota (Winona). St. Teresa, College of. Women. 1903-54. *145*

Franciscans. Archivists. California. Historians. Mission Santa Barbara. 1937-77. *80*

—. California. Historians. Mission Santa Barbara. 1901-77. *79*

—. Clergy. Polish Americans. 1824-91. *144*

Freedmen. Methodists, Northern. Missionaries. Republican Party. South. 1870-73. *87*

Friends, Society of. *American Friend*. Editors. Pennsylvania. Periodicals. 1893-1912. *108*

—. American Revolution (antecedents). Political Attitudes. 1737-77. *165*

—. Antislavery Sentiments. Civil War. Maine. Military Service. 1850's-64. *107*

—. Feminism. Social Reform. ca 1820-80. *150*

—. Friendship. Letters. Pennsylvania. Women. 1778-79. *158*

—. Historiography. 1915-75. *234*

Friendship. Friends, Society of. Letters. Pennsylvania. Women. 1778-79. *158*

—. Mormons. Utah. 1829-68. *111*

Frontier and Pioneer Life. Colorado, northeastern. Methodist Episcopal Church (North, South). Women. 1874-91. *175*

—. Diaries. Missions and Missionaries. Oregon (Forest Grove). Tshimakain Indian Mission. Washington. 1833-97. *243*

Fullmer, Bert E. Adventists. Visions. 1916-29. *194*

Fundamentalism. Baptists. Ontario (Toronto). 1891-1955. *199*

—. North Central States. Populism. Progressivism. 1934-48. *202*

—. Presbyterian Church. Social reform. Washington (Seattle). 1900-40. *134*

G

Gentility (concept). Brattle Street Church. Elites. Massachusetts (Boston). Puritans. 1715-45. *49*

Georgia. Blacks. Church of England. Missions and Missionaries. Political Leadership. Silk industry. 1735-75. *164*

—. Historians. Moravian Church. New York. Pennsylvania, eastern. ca 1735-84. *154*

Georgia (Atlanta). Assimilation. Jews. Rabbis. 1903-70. *78*

Georgia (Valdosta). Blacks. Religious Leaders. 1899-1914. *8*

Gospel music. Clergy. Composers. Methodist Church. 1890's-1958. *16*

Governors. Anglican Communion. Education. Patronage. Philanthropy. Societies. 1686-1728. *156*

Great Awakening. Clergy. Edwards, Jonathan. Evangelism. Missions and Missionaries. 1742-1850's. *28*

—. Connecticut Valley. Massachusetts (Hatfield). Presbyterian Church. 1686-1741. *251*

Great Britain. American Revolution (antecedents). Church of England. Colonial Government. 1773-75. *200*

—. Baptists. Massachusetts (Middleborough). New England. Theology. 1745-65. *6*

—. Beaconites. Bible. Crewdson, Isaac. Quakers. Schisms. 1833-37. *13*

—. Letters. Mormons. Polygamy. Utah (Salt Lake City). Women. 1885-96. *40*

Great Britain (London). Courtship. Indians, Ojibway. Jones, Peter. Methodism. New York. 1820's-33. *71*

Great Plains. Indian-White Relations. Mormons. New York, western. Utah. 1835-51. *257*

Groton School. Episcopal Church, Protestant. Massachusetts. 1884-1940. *170*

H

Hawaii. Andover Theological Seminary. Diaries. Middlebury College. Missions and Missionaries. 1815-39. 21

—. Missions and Missionaries. Occupations. Secularism. 1875-1900. 22

**Henrietta Hebrew Benevolent
Society.** California (San
Bernardino). Charities. Jews.
Women. 1870-91. *2*

Heresy. Episcopal Church,
Protestant. New York
(Rochester). Reform. St.
Andrew's Church. Trials.
1879-1927. *53*

Heretics. Church of England.
Clergy. Connecticut. 1720-82.
14

Hermeneutics. Darwinism.
Episcopal Church, Protestant.
Europe. Excommunications.
Ohio (Canton). St. Paul's
Church. 1890-91. *127*

Hicks, Elias. Ohio. Quakers.
1825-28. *12*

Historians. Archivists.
California. Franciscans.
Mission Santa Barbara. 1937-
77. *80*

—. California. Franciscans.
Mission Santa Barbara. 1901-
77. *79*

—. Clergy. Massachusetts
(Beverly). Rhode Island.
Unitarianism. 1833-47. *215*

—. Georgia. Moravian Church.
New York. Pennsylvania,
eastern. ca 1735-84. *154*

—. Illinois (Bishop Hill).
Preservation. 1875-1919. *217*

Historiography. Friends,
Society of. 1915-75. *234*

—. Mormons. 1913-70. *126*

Holiness Movement Church.
Canada. Evangelism.

Methodist Church. 1887-1921.
96

Homesteaders. Alberta (Red
Deer River area). Missionaries.
Personal narratives.
Saskatchewan. Women. 1905-
64. *30*

Hudson's Bay Company.
Bishops. Canada. Church of
England. Missionaries.
Rupert's Land. 1839-85. *3*

—. Canada, western. Church of
England. Missionaries. 1844-
64. *97*

—. Church of England.
Manitoba (Red River
Settlement). Missionaries.
1823-38. *106*

Humor. Alabama. Bishops.
Catholic Church. 1826-54.
173

I

Icelandic Canadians.
Colonization. Jews. Manitoba.
Refugees. Russia. 1870-90.
229

Idaho (Moscow).
Correspondence courses.
Psychiana (religion). 1929-48.
190

Illinois. Chicago, University of
(Divinity School). Colleges
and Universities. Religious
historians. 1927-46. *222*

Illinois (Bishop Hill).
Historians. Preservation.
1875-1919. *217*

Illinois, central. Canada.
Catholic Church. Clergy.

Illinois (Kankakee area).
Immigrants. Presbyterian
Church. 1830-99. *46*

Illinois (Chicago). Cardinals.
Catholic Church. 20c. *152*

—. Maryland (Baltimore).
Missionaries. Polish
Americans. 1896-1945. *73*

Illinois (Kankakee area).
Canada. Catholic Church.
Clergy. Illinois, central.
Immigrants. Presbyterian
Church. 1830-99. *46*

Illinois (Nauvoo). Family.
Mormons. New York. 1824-
45. *259*

—. Migration, Internal.
Mormons. Utah (Salt Lake
City). 1841-48. *260*

Illinois (Zion). Christian
Catholic Church. Evangelism.
1888-1907. *62*

Immigrants. Canada. Catholic
Church. Clergy. Illinois,
central. Illinois (Kankakee
area). Presbyterian Church.
1830-99. *46*

—. Clergy. Merchants.
Presbyterians. Quebec
(Montreal). Scottish
Canadians. 1824-75. *133*

—. Educators. Midwest.
Swedish Americans. 1873-
1904. *223*

Immigration. Agriculture.
California (San Fernando
Valley). Sheep Raising. 1836-
82. *116*

Immortality (doctrine).
Antinomianism.
Massachusetts. 1638. *98*

Independence Hall. Centennial
Celebrations. Civic affairs.
Pennsylvania (Philadelphia).
Philanthropy. 1793-1882. *197*

India. Educators. Methodist
Church. Missionaries.
Women. Women's Home
Missionary Society. 1865-
1901. *231*

Indians (agencies).
Assimilation. Presbyterian
Church. 1870-82. *123*

Indians, Mohegan. Authors.
Christianity. Missionaries.
1760's-92. *160*

Indians, Ojibway. Courtship.
Great Britain (London). Jones,
Peter. Methodism. New York.
1820's-33. *71*

Indian-White Relations. Blacks.
17c-1792. *15*

—. Great Plains. Mormons.
New York, western. Utah.
1835-51. *257*

—. Methodist Church. Missions
and Missionaries. Wisconsin.
1793-1883. *33*

**Internal Macedonian
Revolutionary Organization.**
American Board
Commissioners for Foreign
Missions. Kidnapping.
Macedonia. Missions and
Missionaries. Roosevelt,
Theodore (administration).
Terrorism. 1901-02. *216*

Inventions. Cotton scrapers. Mississippi. Patent laws. Slavery. ca 1850. *220*

Investments. Massachusetts (Boston, Manchester). Real estate. Transcendentalism. 1850-96. *11*

Iowa (Iowa City). Episcopal Church, Protestant. New York City. Orphans' Home of Industry. 1854-68. *235*

Iowa (Lee County). Land. Mormons. Smith, Joseph. Speculation. 1830's-58. *76*

Ireland. Catholic Church. Fenians. Pennsylvania (Philadelphia). Speeches, Addresses, etc. Wood, James F. 1839-75. *149*

Irish Americans. Canada. Kentucky (Louisville). Leadership. Presbyterian Church. 1858-81. *191*

—. Catholic Church. Minnesota (St. Paul). North Dakota (Jamestown Diocese). 1852-1909. *198*

Irish Canadians. Bishops. Church of Ireland. Ontario. 1861-1901. *118*

J_____

Jefferson, Thomas. American Revolution. Calvinists. Clergy. 1775-1808. *119*

Jesuits. Clergy. Colorado (Conejos). Daily life. Letters. 1874-80. *9*

—. Missionaries. Montana. St. Xavier's Mission. 1887-1906. *174*

—. Personal Narratives. Vatican. World War II. 1942-45. *138*

Jewish studies. Pennsylvania, University of. 1880-1900. *104*

Jewish Theological Seminary. Acculturation. New York City. Theology. 1920's. *109*

Jews. Anti-Zionist sentiment. Colorado (Denver). Patriotism. 1889-1938. *74*

—. Assimilation. Georgia (Atlanta). Rabbis. 1903-70. *78*

—. Assimilation. Zionism. 1914-40's. *148*

—. California. Newspapers. Publishers. Rabbis. San Francisco *Voice of Israel*. San Francisco *Weekly Gleaner*. 1854-61. *19*

—. California (San Bernardino). Charities. Henrietta Hebrew Benevolent Society. Women. 1870-91. *2*

—. California (San Francisco). Missouri (St. Louis). New York City. Pennsylvania (Philadelphia). Rabbis. 1859-82. *238*

—. College Teachers. Discrimination. Johns Hopkins University. Virginia, University of. 1841-77. *224*

—. Colonization. Icelandic Canadians. Manitoba. Refugees. Russia. 1870-90. *229*

—. Conference on Jewish Relations. Philosophy. Values. 1880-1947. *48*

—. Conservatism. Philosophy. Sociology. 1927-77. *90*

—. Educational Reformers. New York City. Social Reformers. Women. 1880-1912. *184*

—. Farmers. Settlement. 1861-1927. *213*

—. Michigan (Detroit). Rabbis. Translating and Interpreting. 1880-1959. *91*

—. Newspapers. Rabbis. 1860-95. *18*

—. North Dakota (Grand Forks). Rabbis. 1890-1934. *166*

Johns Hopkins University. College Teachers. Discrimination. Jews. Virginia, University of. 1841-77. *224*

Jones, Peter. Courtship. Great Britain (London). Indians, Ojibway. Methodism. New York. 1820's-33. *71*

Judaism. Agriculture. Reform. 1880's-1923. *115*

—. California (San Francisco). 1857-69. *89*

Judaism (Orthodox). Canon law. Circumcision. Europe. Louisiana (New Orleans). 1853-65. *99*

Judaism (Reform). California (Los Angeles). 1881-1932. *196*

—. California (Los Angeles). Lawyers. Rabbis. Wilshire

Boulevard Temple. 1895-1927. *211*

—. California (San Francisco). Rabbis. 1873-1908. *241*

—. Leadership. Zionism. 1880-1929. *88*

K

Kansas. Calvinism. First Presbyterian Church of Topeka. Psychology. 1930-80. *141*

Kansas (Topeka). Pentecostalism. Religion. 1873-1929. *167*

Kentucky. Diaries. Missions and Missionaries. North Central States. Presbyterian Church. 1828-45. *180*

Kentucky (Bowling Green). Civil War. Deacons. Episcopalians. Tennessee (Knoxville). 1860-1911. *188*

Kentucky (Louisville). Canada. Irish Americans. Leadership. Presbyterian Church. 1858-81. *191*

Kidnapping. American Board Commissioners for Foreign Missions. Internal Macedonian Revolutionary Organization. Macedonia. Missions and Missionaries. Roosevelt, Theodore (administration). Terrorism. 1901-02. *216*

L

Labour Party. Canada. Communist Party. Methodism. Social Gospel. 1893-1924. *201*

Land. Iowa (Lee County). Mormons. Smith, Joseph. Speculation. 1830's-58. *76*

Language. Baptists. Micmac Indians. Missions and Missionaries. Nova Scotia. 1830-89. *176*

Latin America. Africa. Asia. California. Methodist Church. Missions and Missionaries. 1849-1902. *230*

Lawyers. California (Los Angeles). Judaism (Reform). Rabbis. Wilshire Boulevard Temple. 1895-1927. *211*

Leaders. Mormons. Utah. Women. 1804-87. *209*

Leadership. Canada. Irish Americans. Kentucky (Louisville). Presbyterian Church. 1858-81. *191*

—. Judaism, Reform. Zionism. 1880-1929. *88*

—. Mormons. 1840's-70's. *262*

Lectures. Minnesota (Minneapolis). Norwegian Americans. Unitarianism. 1881-82. *103*

Letters. Catholic Church. Clergy. Pennsylvania (Pittsburgh). 1885-1921. *39*

—. Clergy. Colorado (Conejos). Daily life. Jesuits. 1874-80. 9

—. Daily Life. Missionaries. Oregon. 1840-80. *178*

—. Friends, Society of. Friendship. Pennsylvania. Women. 1778-79. *158*

—. Great Britain. Mormons. Polygamy. Utah (Salt Lake City). Women. 1885-96. *40*

Liberals. Clergy. Missouri (St. Louis). Protestants. Universalists. 1867-1923. *43*

Lopp, W. T. "Tom". Alaska (Cape Prince of Wales). Missions and Missionaries. 1892-1902. *122*

Los Angeles Times. Christianity. Class Struggle. McNamara case. Progressivism. Radicals and Radicalism. 1908-12. *214*

Louisiana. Baptist Historical Society. Publishers and Publishing. 1850-1900. *86*

—. Methodist Episcopal Church. Whig Party. 1843-46. *53*

Louisiana (New Orleans). Canon law. Circumcision. Europe. Judaism (Orthodox). 1853-65. *99*

—. Fiction. Presbyterian Church. ca 1870-1925. *37*

Louisiana (northern). Baptists. Clergy. Social Conditions. 1860-96. *85*

Loyalists. American Revolution. Clergy. Massachusetts (Deerfield). 1766-80. *5*

—. Clergy. Presbyterian Church. 1770-81. *264*

Lutheran Church. African Methodist Episcopal Church. Blacks. Clergy. College Presidents. Wilberforce University. 1830-93. *168*

—. Clergy. New Jersey (Hackensack). 1724-40. *236*

M_____

Macedonia. American Board Commissioners for Foreign Missions. Internal Macedonian Revolutionary Organization. Kidnapping. Missions and Missionaries. Roosevelt, Theodore (administration). Terrorism. 1901-02. *216*

Maine. Antislavery Sentiments. Civil War. Friends, Society of. Military Service. 1850's-64. *107*

Manitoba. Clergy. Farmers. Mennonite Brethren Church. Russian Canadians. 1879-1948. *244*

—. Clergy. Mennonites. Minnesota. Oregon. 1900-53. *242*

—. Colonization. Icelandic Canadians. Jews. Refugees. Russia. 1870-90. *229*

Manitoba (Red River Settlement). Church of England. Hudson's Bay Company. Missionaries. 1823-38. *106*

Maryland. Catholic Church. Church of England. Clergy. 1774-97. *27*

—. Church of England. Clergy. ca 1745-68. *7*

Maryland (Baltimore). Illinois (Chicago). Missionaries. Polish Americans. 1896-1945. *73*

Massachusetts. Antinomianism. Immortality (doctrine). 1638. *98*

—. Church of England. Congregationalism. 1720-30. *56*

—. Episcopal Church, Protestant. Groton School. 1884-1940. *170*

—. Mather, Cotton *(Life of Phips).* Puritans. 1690-1705. *172*

—. Millenarianism. Missionaries. 1604-90. *67*

—. Orientalism. Transcendentalism. Unitarianism. 1840's-82. *105*

—. Philanthropists. 1912-80. *254*

Massachusetts (Beverly). Clergy. Historians. Rhode Island. Unitarianism. 1833-47. *215*

Massachusetts (Boston). Baptists. Blacks. Clergy. 1870's-91. *249*

—. Brattle Street Church. Elites. Gentility (concept). Puritans. 1715-45. *49*

Massachusetts (Boston, Manchester). Investments. Real estate. Transcendentalism. 1850-96. *11*

Massachusetts (Deerfield). American Revolution. Clergy. Loyalists. 1766-80. *5*

Massachusetts (Hatfield). Connecticut Valley. Great

Awakening. Presbyterian Church. 1686-1741. *251*

Massachusetts (Middleborough). Baptists. Great Britain. New England. Theology. 1745-65. *6*

Massachusetts (Northampton). Clergy. Puritans. Sermons. Stoddard, Solomon. 1658-69. *131*

Mather, Cotton (*Life of Phips*). Massachusetts. Puritans. 1690-1705. *172*

McNamara case. Christianity. Class Struggle. *Los Angeles Times*. Progressivism. Radicals and Radicalism. 1908-12. *214*

Mechanics. New Hampshire (Enfield). Shakers. 1829-1923. *55*

Medical Education. Africa. American Colonization Society. Colonization. Presbyterian Church. Slavery. 1840-50. *139*

Mennonite Brethren Church. Clergy. Farmers. Manitoba. Russian Canadians. 1879-1948. *44*

Mennonites. Clergy. Manitoba. Minnesota. Oregon. 1900-53. *242*

Merchant Marine. Bethel Ships. Evangelism. Methodist Church. New York City. Swedish Americans. 1832-66. *17*

Merchants. Clergy. Immigrants. Presbyterians. Quebec (Montreal). Scottish Canadians. 1824-75. *133*

Methodism. Bishops. Missions and Missionaries. Philippines. Singapore. 1854-1937. *161*

—. Canada. Communist Party. Labour Party. Social Gospel. 1893-1924. *201*

—. Congregationalism. Family. Mormons. New England. New York, western. 18c-1830's. *258*

—. Courtship. Great Britain (London). Indians, Ojibway. Jones, Peter. New York. 1820's-33. *71*

Methodist Church. Africa. Asia. California. Latin America. Missions and Missionaries. 1849-1902. *230*

—. Bethel Ships. Evangelism. Merchant Marine. New York City. Swedish Americans. 1832-66. *17*

—. Canada. Evangelism. Holiness Movement Church. 1887-1921. *96*

—. Chautauqua School of Theology. New York. Seminaries, correspondence. 1881-98. *239*

—. Clergy. Composers. Gospel music. 1890's-1958. *16*

—. Educators. India. Missionaries. Women. Women's Home Missionary Society. 1865-1901. *231*

—. Indian-White Relations. Missions and Missionaries. Wisconsin. 1793-1883. *33*

—. Mississippi (Natchez area). 1810. *252*

Methodist Episcopal Church. Louisiana. Whig Party. 1843-46. *253*

Methodist Episcopal Church, African. Blacks. Clergy. New York City. 1787-1875. *60*

Methodist Episcopal Church (North, South). Colorado, northeastern. Frontier and Pioneer Life. Women. 1874-91. *175*

Methodist Episcopal Church (South). Mississippi. Religious Education. 1841-60. *232*

Methodist Protestant Church. Autobiography. Clergy. Daily Life. Delaware (Sussex County). 1780-1857. *146*

Methodists. Autobiography. Clergy. 1810's-50's. *41*

—. Canada. Clergy. 1880-86. *24*

Methodists, Northern. Freedmen. Missionaries. Republican Party. South. 1870-73. *87*

Michigan (Beaver Island). Mormons. Polygamy. Wisconsin (Voree). 1830-55. *218*

Michigan (Detroit). Jews. Rabbis. Translating and Interpreting. 1880-1959. *91*

Micmac Indians. Baptists. Language. Missions and

Missionaries. Nova Scotia. 1830-89. *176*

Middlebury College. Andover Theological Seminary. Diaries. Hawaii. Missions and Missionaries. 1815-39. *21*

Midwest. Authors. Clergy. Disciples of Christ. Pennsylvania. 1896-1908. *256*

—. Educators. Immigrants. Swedish Americans. 1873-1904. *223*

Migration, Internal. Illinois (Nauvoo). Mormons. Utah (Salt Lake City). 1841-48. *260*

Military Service. Antislavery Sentiments. Civil War. Friends, Society of. Maine. 1850's-64. *107*

Millenarianism. Benedictines. Catholic Church. 1837-69. *208*

—. Massachusetts. Missionaries. 1604-90. *67*

Mining. Mormons. Utah. 1814-69. *181*

Minnesota. Catholic Church. Educators. Sisters of St. Joseph of Corondelet. 1842-1930. *101*

—. Clergy. Manitoba. Mennonites. Oregon. 1900-53. *242*

Minnesota (Minneapolis). Lectures. Norwegian Americans. Unitarianism. 1881-82. *103*

Minnesota, northern. Diaries. Missionaries. Wisconsin. 1833-49. *69*

Minnesota (St. Paul). Catholic Church. Irish Americans. North Dakota (Jamestown Diocese). 1852-1909. *198*

Minnesota (Winona). Catholic Church. Franciscan Sisters. St. Teresa, College of. Women. 1903-54. *145*

Mission Santa Barbara. Archivists. California. Franciscans. Historians. 1937-77. *80*

—. California. Catholic Church. Missionaries. Southwestern history. 1851-1934. *70*

—. California. Franciscans. Historians. 1901-77. *79*

Missionaries. Alberta (Red Deer River area). Homesteaders. Personal narratives. Saskatchewan. Women. 1905-64. *30*

—. Authors. Christianity. Indians, Mohegan. 1760's-92. *160*

—. Bishops. Canada. Church of England. Hudson's Bay Company. Rupert's Land. 1839-85. *3*

—. Black Hills. Episcopal Church, Protestant. 1860-76. *92*

—. California. Catholic Church. Mission Santa Barbara. Southwestern history. 1851-1934. *70*

—. Calvinistic Methodist Church. Nebraska, eastern. 1853-60. *57*

—. Canada, western. Church of England. Hudson's Bay Company. 1844-64. *97*

—. Church of England. Hudson's Bay Company. Manitoba (Red River Settlement). 1823-38. *106*

—. Clergy. Nova Scotia (Lunenburg). St. John's Anglican Church. 1814-25. *1*

—. Congregational Church. South Dakota (Oahe). 1875-1910. 50

—. Daily Life. Letters. Oregon. 1840-80. *178*

—. Diaries. Minnesota, northern. Wisconsin. 1833-49. *69*

—. Educators. India. Methodist Church. Women. Women's Home Missionary Society. 1865-1901. *231*

—. Freedmen. Methodists, Northern. Republican Party. South. 1870-73. 87

—. Illinois (Chicago). Maryland (Baltimore). Polish Americans. 1896-1945. *73*

—. Jesuits. Montana. St. Xavier's Mission. 1887-1906. *174*

—. Massachusetts. Millenarianism. 1604-90. *67*

—. Nova Scotia. Sierra Leone (Sherbro Island). Slaves. 1839-50. *179*

Missions and Missionaries.
Africa. Asia. California. Latin
America. Methodist Church.
1849-1902. *230*

—. Alaska (Cape Prince of
Wales). Lopp, W. T. ""Tom''.
1892-1902. *122*

—. Allegheny Mountains.
Catholic Church. Clergy.
Pennsylvania, western. 1799-
1840. *77*

—. American Board
Commissioners for Foreign
Missions. Internal Macedonian
Revolutionary Organization.
Kidnapping. Macedonia.
Roosevelt, Theodore
(administration). Terrorism.
1901-02. *216*

—. American Missionary
Association. Blacks. New
York. Reconstruction. South.
Teachers. 1865-77. *143*

—. Andover Theological
Seminary. Diaries. Hawaii.
Middlebury College. 1815-39.
21

—. Art criticism. California.
Catholic Church. 1769-1980.
157

—. Baptists. Language. Micmac
Indians. Nova Scotia. 1830-
89. *176*

—. Baptists. Oklahoma (Wichita
Mountains). Women's
American Baptist Home
Missionary Society. 1893-
1961. *54*

—. Belgian Congo. Presbyterian
Church (Southern). 1895-98.
237

—. Bishops. Methodism.
Philippines. Singapore. 1854-
1937. *161*

—. Blacks. Church of England.
Georgia. Political Leadership.
Silk industry. 1735-75. *164*

—. California (San Francisco).
Chinese Americans.
Presbyterian Mission Home.
Women. 1869-1920. *38*

—. Cape Verde Islands. North
Carolina. Poetry. 1752-62.
205

—. Church of England. Ontario
(Moosonee). 1835-1910. *240*

—. Clergy. Edwards, Jonathan.
Evangelism. Great Awakening.
1742-1850's. *28*

—. Congregationalism.
Converts. Family. Vermont.
1789-1819. *20*

—. Congregationalism.
Nationalism. Social Gospel.
Wyoming (Cheyenne). 1871-
1916. *219*

—. Diaries. Frontier and Pioneer
Life. Oregon (Forest Grove).
Tshimakain Indian Mission.
Washington. 1833-97. *243*

—. Diaries. Kentucky. North
Central States. Presbyterian
Church. 1828-45. *180*

—. Documents. Western States.
1850-72. *120*

—. Hawaii. Occupations.
Secularism. 1875-1900. *22*

—. Indian-White Relations.
Methodist Church. Wisconsin.
1793-1883. *33*

—. Mississippi (Mayhew Mission). Oklahoma, southeastern. 1820-68. *36*

—. New Mexico (Trementina). Presbyterian Church. 1910-50. *23*

—. Presbyterian Church. 1834-1909. *102*

—. Southern Baptist Theological Seminary. 1859-1954. *42*

Mississippi. Cotton scrapers. Inventions. Patent laws. Slavery. ca 1850. *220*

—. Methodist Episcopal Church (South). Religious Education. 1841-60. *232*

Mississippi (Mayhew Mission). Missions and Missionaries. Oklahoma, southeastern. 1820-68. *36*

Mississippi (Natchez area). Methodist Church. 1810. *252*

Missouri (St. Louis). California (San Francisco). Jews. New York City. Pennsylvania (Philadelphia). Rabbis. 1859-82. *238*

—. Clergy. Liberals. Protestants. Universalists. 1867-1923. *43*

Montana. Clergy. Presbyterian Church. Sunday schools. Travel. 1870's-1927. *68*

—. Jesuits. Missionaries. St. Xavier's Mission. 1887-1906. *174*

Moravian Church. Georgia. Historians. New York.

Pennsylvania, eastern. ca 1735-84. *154*

Mormon Relief Society (Social Services Department). Charities. Utah. 1919-29. *125*

Mormons. 1801-77. 1977. *261*

—. Agricultural College of Utah, Logan. Brigham Young College. Colleges and Universities. Educational Administrators. State Politics. Utah. 1894-1907. *110*

—. Apostasy. 1959-82. *228*

—. Biography. 1943-78. *112*

—. Bishops. Episcopal Church, Protestant. Social Change. Utah. 1905-14. *212*

—. *Book of Mormon.* Exegesis. Theology. 1823-1984. *189*

—. Church of Christ. Church of Jesus Christ of the Children of Zion. 1844-76. *185*

—. Clergy. 1830-45. *207*

—. Clergy. 1833-93. *206*

—. Clergy. Theology. 1834-73. *124*

—. Congregationalism. Family. Methodism. New England. New York, western. 18c-1830's. *258*

—. Converts. Negroes. Slavery. Utah (Salt Lake City). 1844-76. *44*

—. Education. Science. 1876-84. *226*

—. Family. Illinois (Nauvoo). New York. 1824-45. *259*

—. Friendship. Utah. 1829-68. *111*

—. Great Britain. Letters. Polygamy. Utah (Salt Lake City). Women. 1885-96. *40*

—. Great Plains. Indian-White Relations. New York, western. Utah. 1835-51. *257*

—. Historiography. 1913-70. *126*

—. Illinois (Nauvoo). Migration, Internal. Utah (Salt Lake City). 1841-48. *260*

—. Iowa (Lee County). Land. Smith, Joseph. Speculation. 1830's-58. *76*

—. Leaders. Utah. Women. 1804-87. *209*

—. Leadership. 1840's-70's. *262*

—. Michigan (Beaver Island). Polygamy. Wisconsin (Voree). 1830-55. *218*

—. Mining. Utah. 1814-69. *181*

—. Photographers. Utah, southern. 1877-1928. *4*

—. Suffrage. Women. ca 1870-1910. *248*

—. Theology. ca 1800-44. *204*

—. Utah. 1840's-81. *245*

—. Utah. 1846-1909. *82*

—. Women, status of. 1830-90. *210*

Musicians. Christian Science. Educators. 1856-1938. *263*

N

Nationalism. Congregationalism. Missions and Missionaries. Social Gospel. Wyoming (Cheyenne). 1871-1916. *219*

Nebraska, eastern. Calvinistic Methodist Church. Missionaries. 1853-60. *57*

Negroes. Converts. Mormons. Slavery. Utah (Salt Lake City). 1844-76. *44*

New England. Baptists. Great Britain. Massachusetts (Middleborough). Theology. 1745-65. *6*

—. Congregationalism. Family. Methodism. Mormons. New York, western. 18c-1830's. *258*

New Hampshire (Enfield). Mechanics. Shakers. 1829-1923. *55*

New Jersey. American Revolution. Politics. Religion. 1770-90. *83*

New Jersey (Hackensack). Clergy. Lutheran Church. 1724-40. *236*

New Lights. Alline, Henry. Nova Scotia. Sects, Religious. 1769-1834. *169*

New Mexico (Trementina). Missions and Missionaries. Presbyterian Church. 1910-50. *23*

New Thought. Faith healing. Southwest. 1893-97. *195*

New York. American Missionary Association.

Blacks. Missions and Missionaries. Reconstruction. South. Teachers. 1865-77. *143*

—. Chautauqua School of Theology. Methodist Church. Seminaries, correspondence. 1881-98. *239*

—. Courtship. Great Britain (London). Indians, Ojibway. Jones, Peter. Methodism. 1820's-33. *71*

—. Family. Illinois (Nauvoo). Mormons. 1824-45. *259*

—. Georgia. Historians. Moravian Church. Pennsylvania, eastern. ca 1735-84. *154*

—. Presbyterian Church. Schisms. Theology. Union Theological Seminary. 1865-70. *203*

New York City. Acculturation. Jewish Theological Seminary. Theology. 1920's. *109*

—. Bethel Ships. Evangelism. Merchant Marine. Methodist Church. Swedish Americans. 1832-66. *17*

—. Blacks. Clergy. Methodist Episcopal Church, African. 1787-1875. *60*

—. California (San Francisco). Jews. Missouri (St. Louis). Pennsylvania (Philadelphia). Rabbis. 1859-82. *238*

—. Educational Reformers. Jews. Social Reformers. Women. 1880-1912. *184*

—. Episcopal Church, Protestant. Iowa (Iowa City). Orphans'Home of Industry. 1854-68. *235*

—. Retrenchment Society. Sects, Religious. 1828-35. *136*

—. Zionism. 1900-12. *128*

New York (Hyde Park). Church administrators. Presidents. St. James Episcopal Church. 1933-45. *192*

New York (Rochester). Episcopal Church, Protestant. Heresy. Reform. St. Andrew's Church. Trials. 1879-1927. *53*

—. Norwegian Americans. Quakers. 1807-44. *117*

New York, western. Congregationalism. Family. Methodism. Mormons. New England. 18c-1830's. *258*

—. Great Plains. Indian-White Relations. Mormons. Utah. 1835-51. *257*

Newspapers. California. Jews. Publishers. Rabbis. San Francisco *Voice of Israel*. San Francisco *Weekly Gleaner*. 1854-61. *19*

—. Jews. Rabbis. 1860-95. *18*

North Carolina. Cape Verde Islands. Missions and Missionaries. Poetry. 1752-62. *205*

North Central States. Diaries. Kentucky. Missions and Missionaries. Presbyterian Church. 1828-45. *180*

—. Fundamentalism. Populism. Progressivism. 1934-48. *202*

North Dakota (Grand Forks). Jews. Rabbis. 1890-1934. *166*

North Dakota (Jamestown Diocese). Catholic Church. Irish Americans. Minnesota (St. Paul). 1852-1909. *198*

Norwegian Americans. Lectures. Minnesota (Minneapolis). Unitarianism. 1881-82. *103*

—. New York (Rochester). Quakers. 1807-44. *117*

Nova Scotia. Alline, Henry. New Lights. Sects, Religious. 1769-1834. *169*

—. Baptists. Language. Micmac Indians. Missions and Missionaries. 1830-89. *176*

—. Missionaries. Sierra Leone (Sherbro Island). Slaves. 1839-50. *179*

Nova Scotia (Lunenburg). Clergy. Missionaries. St. John's Anglican Church. 1814-25. *1*

O

Occupations. Hawaii. Missions and Missionaries. Secularism. 1875-1900. *22*

Ohio. Hicks, Elias. Quakers. 1825-28. *12*

Ohio (Canton). Darwinism. Episcopal Church, Protestant. Europe. Excommunications. Hermeneutics. St. Paul's Church. 1890-91. *127*

Ohio (Warren). Baptists. 1817-22. *186*

Oklahoma, southeastern. Missions and Missionaries. Mississippi (Mayhew Mission). 1820-68. *36*

Oklahoma (Wichita Mountains). Baptists. Missions and Missionaries. Women's American Baptist Home Missionary Society. 1893-1961. *54*

Ontario. Bishops. Church of Ireland. Irish Canadians. 1861-1901. *118*

Ontario (Moosonee). Church of England. Missions and Missionaries. 1835-1910. *240*

Ontario (Toronto). Baptists. Fundamentalism. 1891-1955. *199*

Oregon. Clergy. Manitoba. Mennonites. Minnesota. 1900-53. *242*

—. Daily Life. Letters. Missionaries. 1840-80. *178*

Oregon (Forest Grove). Diaries. Frontier and Pioneer Life. Missions and Missionaries. Tshimakain Indian Mission. Washington. 1833-97. *243*

Orientalism. Massachusetts. Transcendentalism. Unitarianism. 1840's-82. *105*

Orphans' Home of Industry. Episcopal Church, Protestant. Iowa (Iowa City). New York City. 1854-68. *235*

P

Pacific Northwest. Charity of Providence, Sisters of. Construction. Pioneers. 1856-1902. *129*

Patent laws. Cotton scrapers. Inventions. Mississippi. Slavery. ca 1850. *220*

Patriotism. Anti-Zionist sentiment. Colorado (Denver). Jews. 1889-1938. *74*

Patronage. Anglican Communion. Education. Governors. Philanthropy. Societies. 1686-1728. *156*

Peace. Conflict. Philosophy. 1630-84. *250*

Pennsylvania. *American Friend.* Editors. Friends, Society of. Periodicals. 1893-1912. *108*

—. Authors. Clergy. Disciples of Christ. Midwest. 1896-1908. *256*

—. Friends, Society of. Friendship. Letters. Women. 1778-79. *158*

—. Personality. Religion. Settlement. 1660-1700. *171*

Pennsylvania, eastern. Georgia. Historians. Moravian Church. New York. ca 1735-84. *154*

Pennsylvania (Philadelphia). California (San Francisco). Jews. Missouri (St. Louis). New York City. Rabbis. 1859-82. *238*

—. Catholic Church. Fenians. Ireland. Speeches, Addresses,

etc. Wood, James F. 1839-75. *149*

—. Centennial Celebrations. Civic affairs. Independence Hall. Philanthropy. 1793-1882. *197*

Pennsylvania (Pittsburgh). Catholic Church. Clergy. Letters. 1885-1921. *39*

Pennsylvania, University of. Jewish studies. 1880-1900. *104*

Pennsylvania, western. Allegheny Mountains. Catholic Church. Clergy. Missions and Missionaries. 1799-1840. *77*

Pentecostalism. Kansas (Topeka). Religion. 1873-1929. *167*

Periodicals. *American Friend.* Editors. Friends, Society of. Pennsylvania. 1893-1912. *108*

Personal narratives. Alberta (Red Deer River area). Homesteaders. Missionaries. Saskatchewan. Women. 1905-64. *30*

—. Jesuits. Vatican. World War II. 1942-45. *138*

Personality. Christian Science. Shakers. Theology. 1736-1910. *64*

—. Pennsylvania. Religion. Settlement. 1660-1700. *171*

Philanthropists. Massachusetts. 1912-80. *254*

Philanthropy. Anglican Communion. Education.

Governors. Patronage. Societies. 1686-1728. *156*

—. Centennial Celebrations. Civic affairs. Independence Hall. Pennsylvania (Philadelphia). 1793-1882. *197*

Philippines. Bishops. Methodism. Missions and Missionaries. Singapore. 1854-1937. *161*

Philosophy. Conference on Jewish Relations. Jews. Values. 1880-1947. *48*

—. Conflict. Peace. 1630-84. *250*

—. Conservatism. Jews. Sociology. 1927-77. *90*

Photographers. Mormons. Utah, southern. 1877-1928. *4*

Pioneers. Charity of Providence, Sisters of. Construction. Pacific Northwest. 1856-1902. *129*

Plymouth Church. Congregationalists. Social Gospel. Wisconsin (Milwaukee). 1880-1915. *233*

Poetry. Canada. Dukhobors. 1909-67. *225*

—. Cape Verde Islands. Missions and Missionaries. North Carolina. 1752-62. *205*

Polish Americans. Catholic Church. Clergy. 1863-1913. *114*

—. Clergy. Franciscans. 1824-91. *144*

—. Illinois (Chicago). Maryland (Baltimore). Missionaries. 1896-1945. *73*

Political Attitudes. American Revolution (antecedents). Friends, Society of. 1737-77. *165*

Political Leadership. Blacks. Church of England. Georgia. Missions and Missionaries. Silk industry. 1735-75. *164*

—. Presbyterian Church. 1772-1805. *34*

Politics. American Revolution. New Jersey. Religion. 1770-90. *83*

—. American Revolution (antecedents). Church and state. Connecticut. Theologians. 1714-71. *59*

—. Baptists. Conservatism. First Baptist Church (Fort Worth). Texas. 1900-50. *159*

Polygamy. Great Britain. Letters. Mormons. Utah (Salt Lake City). Women. 1885-96. *40*

—. Michigan (Beaver Island). Mormons. Wisconsin (Voree). 1830-55. *218*

Populism. Fundamentalism. North Central States. Progressivism. 1934-48. *202*

Presbyterian Church. 1900-38. *255*

—. Africa. American Colonization Society. Colonization. Medical Education. Slavery. 1840-50. *139*

—. Assimilation. Indians (agencies). 1870-82. *123*

—. Blacks. South. 1930-75. *26*

—. Canada. Catholic Church. Clergy. Illinois, central. Illinois (Kankakee area). Immigrants. 1830-99. *46*

—. Canada. Irish Americans. Kentucky (Louisville). Leadership. 1858-81. *191*

—. Church and State. Church of England (opposition to). ca 1750-90. *121*

—. Clergy. Loyalists. 1770-81. *264*

—. Clergy. Montana. Sunday schools. Travel. 1870's-1927. *68*

—. Connecticut Valley. Great Awakening. Massachusetts (Hatfield). 1686-1741. *251*

—. Diaries. Kentucky. Missions and Missionaries. North Central States. 1828-45. *180*

—. Ecumenism. Evangelical and Reformed Church. World Alliance of Reformed Churches. 1900-55. *182*

—. Fiction. Louisiana (New Orleans). ca 1870-1925. *37*

—. Fundamentalism. Social reform. Washington (Seattle). 1900-40. *134*

—. Missions and Missionaries. 1834-1909. *102*

—. Missions and Missionaries. New Mexico (Trementina). 1910-50. *23*

—. New York. Schisms. Theology. Union Theological Seminary. 1865-70. *203*

—. Political Leadership. 1772-1805. *34*

Presbyterian Church, New School. Ecumenism. Slavery issue. 1840's. *52*

Presbyterian Church, Reformed. Antislavery Sentiments. Clergy. Vermont (Ryegate). 1785-1820. *142*

Presbyterian Church (Southern). Belgian Congo. Missions and Missionaries. 1895-98. *237*

Presbyterian Mission Home. California (San Francisco). Chinese Americans. Missions and Missionaries. Women. 1869-1920. *38*

Presbyterians. Chaplains. Scholars. Teachers. 1770's-1809. *137*

—. Clergy. Immigrants. Merchants. Quebec (Montreal). Scottish Canadians. 1824-75. *133*

Preservation. Historians. Illinois (Bishop Hill). 1875-1919. *217*

Presidents. Church administrators. New York (Hyde Park). St. James Episcopal Church. 1933-45. *192*

Priests. *Alaska Herald*. Editors. Far Western States. Ukrainian Americans. 1832-1916. *93*

Progressivism. Christianity. Class Struggle. *Los Angeles Times*. McNamara case. Radicals and Radicalism. 1908-12. *214*

—. Fundamentalism. North Central States. Populism. 1934-48. *202*

Protestantism. 1869-1902. *227*

—. Canada. 1866-1960. *221*

—. Catholic Church. Ecumenism. 1950-64. *247*

—. Clergy. 1895-1950. *155*

Protestants. Clergy. Liberals. Missouri (St. Louis). Universalists. 1867-1923. *43*

Psychiana (religion). Correspondence courses. Idaho (Moscow). 1929-48. *190*

Psychology. Calvinism. First Presbyterian Church of Topeka. Kansas. 1930-80. *141*

Publishers. California. Jews. Newspapers. Rabbis. San Francisco *Voice of Israel*. San Francisco *Weekly Gleaner*. 1854-61. *19*

Publishers and Publishing. Baptist Historical Society. Louisiana. 1850-1900. *86*

—. Civil War. Reconstruction. State Politics. Tennessee. Unionists. 1825-77. *32*

Puritans. Brattle Street Church. Elites. Gentility (concept). Massachusetts (Boston). 1715-45. *49*

—. Clergy. Massachusetts (Northampton). Sermons.

Stoddard, Solomon. 1658-69. *131*

—. Massachusetts. Mather, Cotton *(Life of Phips)*. 1690-1705. *172*

Q

Quakers. Beaconites. Bible. Crewdson, Isaac. Great Britain. Schisms. 1833-37. *213*

—. Hicks, Elias. Ohio. 1825-28. *12*

—. New York (Rochester). Norwegian Americans. 1807-44. *117*

Quebec. Apostolic Delegates. Catholic Church. 1877-78. *51*

Quebec (Montreal). Clergy. Immigrants. Merchants. Presbyterians. Scottish Canadians. 1824-75. *133*

R

Rabbis. Assimilation. Georgia (Atlanta). Jews. 1903-70. *78*

—. California. Jews. Newspapers. Publishers. San Francisco *Voice of Israel*. San Francisco *Weekly Gleaner*. 1854-61. *19*

—. California (Los Angeles). Judaism (Reform). Lawyers. Wilshire Boulevard Temple. 1895-1927. *211*

—. California (San Francisco). Jews. Missouri (St. Louis). New York City. Pennsylvania (Philadelphia). 1859-82. *238*

—. California (San Francisco).
Judaism (Reform). 1873-1908.
241

—. Jews. Michigan (Detroit).
Translating and Interpreting.
1880-1959. *91*

—. Jews. Newspapers. 1860-95.
18

—. Jews. North Dakota (Grand
Forks). 1890-1934. *166*

Race Relations. Attitudes.
Bermuda. Blacks. Canada.
Church of England. Feild,
Edward. 1825-50. *100*

Radicals and Radicalism.
Christianity. Class Struggle.
Los Angeles Times.
McNamara case.
Progressivism. 1908-12. *214*

Real estate. Investments.
Massachusetts (Boston,
Manchester).
Transcendentalism. 1850-96.
11

Reconstruction. American
Missionary Association.
Blacks. Missions and
Missionaries. New York.
South. Teachers. 1865-77.
143

—. Civil War. Episcopal
Church, Protestant. Theology.
1860-1914. *63*

—. Civil War. Publishers and
Publishing. State Politics.
Tennessee. Unionists. 1825-
77. *32*

Reform. Agriculture. Judaism.
1880's-1923. *115*

—. Episcopal Church, Protestant.
Heresy. New York
(Rochester). St. Andrew's
Church. Trials. 1879-1927.
53

Refugees. Colonization.
Icelandic Canadians. Jews.
Manitoba. Russia. 1870-90.
229

Religious Education. Clergy.
1775. *84*

—. Evangelism. 1807-52. *163*

—. Methodist Episcopal Church
(South). Mississippi. 1841-60.
232

Religious historians. Chicago,
University of (Divinity
School). Colleges and
Universities. Illinois. 1927-46.
222

Religious Leaders. Blacks.
Georgia (Valdosta). 1899-
1914. *8*

Retrenchment Society. New
York City. Sects, Religious.
1828-35. *136*

Revivals. Calvinists.
Theologians. 1719-1850. *132*

Rhode Island. Clergy.
Historians. Massachusetts
(Beverly). Unitarianism.
1833-47. *215*

Rhode Island (Newport).
American Revolution.
Antislavery Sentiments.
Congregationalism. ca 1770-
1803. *95*

Rites and Ceremonies. Catholic
Church. Episcopal Church,

Protestant. Vermont. 1832-68.
94

**Roosevelt, Theodore
(administration).** American
Board Commissioners for
Foreign Missions. Internal
Macedonian Revolutionary
Organization. Kidnapping.
Macedonia. Missions and
Missionaries. Terrorism.
1901-02. *216*

Rupert's Land. Bishops.
Canada. Church of England.
Hudson's Bay Company.
Missionaries. 1839-85. *3*

Russia. Colonization. Icelandic
Canadians. Jews. Manitoba.
Refugees. 1870-90. *229*

Russian Canadians. Clergy.
Farmers. Manitoba.
Mennonite Brethren Church.
1879-1948. *244*

S_____

St. Andrew's Church. Episcopal
Church, Protestant. Heresy.
New York (Rochester).
Reform. Trials. 1879-1927.
53

St. James Episcopal Church.
Church administrators. New
York (Hyde Park). Presidents.
1933-45. *192*

St. John's Anglican Church.
Clergy. Missionaries. Nova
Scotia (Lunenburg). 1814-25.
1

St. Paul's Church. Darwinism.
Episcopal Church, Protestant.
Europe. Excommunications.

Hermeneutics. Ohio (Canton).
1890-91. *127*

St. Teresa, College of. Catholic
Church. Franciscan Sisters.
Minnesota (Winona). Women.
1903-54. *145*

St. Xavier's Mission. Jesuits.
Missionaries. Montana. 1887-
1906. *174*

San Francisco *Voice of Israel.*
California. Jews. Newspapers.
Publishers. Rabbis. San
Francisco *Weekly Gleaner.*
1854-61. *19*

San Francisco *Weekly Gleaner.*
California. Jews. Newspapers.
Publishers. Rabbis. San
Francisco *Voice of Israel.*
1854-61. *19*

Saskatchewan. Alberta (Red
Deer River area).
Homesteaders. Missionaries.
Personal narratives. Women.
1905-64. *30*

Schisms. Beaconites. Bible.
Crewdson, Isaac. Great
Britain. Quakers. 1833-37. *13*

—. New York. Presbyterian
Church. Theology. Union
Theological Seminary. 1865-
70. *203*

Scholars. Chaplains.
Presbyterians. Teachers.
1770's-1809. *137*

Science. Clergy. Theology.
1866-1900. 193

—. Education. Mormons. 1876-
84. *226*

Scottish Canadians. Clergy.
Immigrants. Merchants.

Presbyterians. Quebec (Montreal). 1824-75. *133*

Sects, Religious. Alline, Henry. New Lights. Nova Scotia. 1769-1834. *169*

—. New York City. Retrenchment Society. 1828-35. *136*

Secularism. Hawaii. Missions and Missionaries. Occupations. 1875-1900. *22*

Seminaries, correspondence. Chautauqua School of Theology. Methodist Church. New York. 1881-98. *239*

Sermons. Clergy. Massachusetts (Northampton). Puritans. Stoddard, Solomon. 1658-69. *131*

Settlement. Farmers. Jews. 1861-1927. *213*

—. Pennsylvania. Personality. Religion. 1660-1700. *171*

Shakers. Christian Science. Personality. Theology. 1736-1910. *64*

—. Mechanics. New Hampshire (Enfield). 1829-1923. *55*

Sheep Raising. Agriculture. California (San Fernando Valley). Immigration. 1836-82. *116*

Siam. Baptists (American). China. 1865-90. *72*

Sierra Leone (Sherbro Island). Missionaries. Nova Scotia. Slaves. 1839-50. *179*

Silk industry. Blacks. Church of England. Georgia. Missions

and Missionaries. Political Leadership. 1735-75. *164*

Singapore. Bishops. Methodism. Missions and Missionaries. Philippines. 1854-1937. *161*

Sioux Indians. Catholic Church. South Dakota. Yankton Reservation (Marty Mission). 1918-49. *66*

Sisters of St. Joseph of Corondelet. Catholic Church. Educators. Minnesota. 1842-1930. *101*

Slavery. Africa. American Colonization Society. Colonization. Medical Education. Presbyterian Church. 1840-50. *139*

—. Converts. Mormons. Negroes. Utah (Salt Lake City). 1844-76. *44*

—. Cotton scrapers. Inventions. Mississippi. Patent laws. ca 1850. *220*

Slavery issue. Ecumenism. Presbyterian Church, New School. 1840's. *52*

Slaves. Missionaries. Nova Scotia. Sierra Leone (Sherbro Island). 1839-50. *179*

Smith, Joseph. Iowa (Lee County). Land. Mormons. Speculation. 1830's-58. *76*

Social Change. Bishops. Episcopal Church, Protestant. Mormons. Utah. 1905-14. *212*

Social Conditions. Baptists.
Clergy. Louisiana (northern).
1860-96. *85*

Social Gospel. Blacks. Clergy.
Socialism. 1880's-90's. *177*

—. Canada. Communist Party.
Labour Party. Methodism.
1893-1924. *201*

—. Congregationalism. Missions
and Missionaries. Nationalism.
Wyoming (Cheyenne). 1871-
1916. *219*

—. Congregationalists.
Plymouth Church. Wisconsin
(Milwaukee). 1880-1915. *233*

Social psychology. Religion.
1890's-1931. *140*

Social Reform. Clergy. First
Presbyterian Church.
Washington (Seattle). 1880's-
1920. *135*

—. Feminism. Friends, Society
of. ca 1820-80. *150*

—. Fundamentalism.
Presbyterian Church.
Washington (Seattle). 1900-40.
134

Social Reformers. Educational
Reformers. Jews. New York
City. Women. 1880-1912.
184

Socialism. Blacks. Clergy.
Social Gospel. 1880's-90's.
177

Societies. Anglican Communion.
Education. Governors.
Patronage. Philanthropy.
1686-1728. *156*

Society of the Atonement.
Catholic Church. Church Unity
Octave. Ecumenists.
Episcopal Church, Protestant.
1908-40. *246*

Sociology. Conservatism. Jews.
Philosophy. 1927-77. *90*

South. American Missionary
Association. Blacks. Missions
and Missionaries. New York.
Reconstruction. Teachers.
1865-77. *143*

—. Blacks. Presbyterian Church.
1930-75. *26*

—. Freedmen. Methodists,
Northern. Missionaries.
Republican Party. 1870-73. *87*

South Dakota. Catholic Church.
Sioux Indians. Yankton
Reservation (Marty Mission).
1918-49. *66*

South Dakota (Oahe).
Congregational Church.
Missionaries. 1875-1910. *50*

South or Southern States.
Chaplains, Army. Civil War.
Episcopal Church, Protestant.
1851-72. *10*

**Southern Baptist Theological
Seminary.** Missions and
Missionaries. 1859-1954. *42*

Southwest. Faith healing. New
Thought. 1893-97. *195*

Southwestern history.
California. Catholic Church.
Mission Santa Barbara.
Missionaries. 1851-1934. *70*

Speculation. Iowa (Lee County).
Land. Mormons. Smith,
Joseph. 1830's-58. *76*

Speeches, Addresses, etc.
Catholic Church. Fenians.
Ireland. Pennsylvania
(Philadelphia). Wood, James
F. 1839-75. *149*

State Politics. Agricultural
College of Utah, Logan.
Brigham Young College.
Colleges and Universities.
Educational Administrators.
Mormons. Utah. 1894-1907.
110

—. Civil War. Publishers and
Publishing. Reconstruction.
Tennessee. Unionists. 1825-
77. *32*

Statesmen. Canada. Clergy.
Educators. 1902-35. *162*

Stoddard, Solomon. Clergy.
Massachusetts (Northampton).
Puritans. Sermons. 1658-69.
131

Suffrage. Mormons. Women.
ca 1870-1910. *248*

Sunday schools. Clergy.
Montana. Presbyterian Church.
Travel. 1870's-1927. *68*

Supreme Court. Church and
State. 1949-67. *47*

Supreme Court Justices.
Catholic Church. 19c-20c. *35*

Swedish Americans. Bethel
Ships. Evangelism. Merchant
Marine. Methodist Church.
New York City. 1832-66. *17*

—. Educators. Immigrants.
Midwest. 1873-1904. *223*

T_____

Teachers. American Missionary
Association. Blacks. Missions
and Missionaries. New York.
Reconstruction. South. 1865-
77. *143*

—. Chaplains. Presbyterians.
Scholars. 1770's-1809. *137*

Temperance Movements.
Editors and Editing.
Tennessee. *Whig* (newspaper).
1838-51. *31*

Tennessee. Civil War.
Publishers and Publishing.
Reconstruction. State Politics.
Unionists. 1825-77. *32*

—. Editors and Editing.
Temperance Movements. *Whig*
(newspaper). 1838-51. *31*

Tennessee (Knoxville). Civil
War. Deacons. Episcopalians.
Kentucky (Bowling Green).
1860-1911. *188*

Terrorism. American Board
Commissioners for Foreign
Missions. Internal
Macedonian Revolutionary
Organization. Kidnapping.
Macedonia. Missions and
Missionaries. Roosevelt,
Theodore (administration).
1901-02. *216*

Texas. Baptists. Conservatism.
First Baptist Church (Fort
Worth). Politics. 1900-50.
159

Theologians. American
Revolution (antecedents).
Church and state. Connecticut.
Politics. 1714-71. *59*

—. Calvinists. Revivals. 1719-1850. *132*

Theology. Acculturation. Jewish Theological Seminary. New York City. 1920's. *109*

—. Baptists. Great Britain. Massachusetts (Middleborough). New England. 1745-65. *6*

—. *Book of Mormon*. Exegesis. Mormons. 1823-1984. *189*

—. Christian Science. Personality. Shakers. 1736-1910. *64*

—. Civil War. Episcopal Church, Protestant. Reconstruction. 1860-1914. *63*

—. Clergy. Mormons. 1834-73. *124*

—. Clergy. Science. 1866-1900. *193*

—. Mormons. ca 1800-44. *204*

—. New York. Presbyterian Church. Schisms. Union Theological Seminary. 1865-70. *203*

—. Transcendentalism. 1830-90. *75*

Transcendentalism. Investments. Massachusetts (Boston, Manchester). Real estate. 1850-96. *11*

—. Massachusetts. Orientalism. Unitarianism. 1840's-82. *105*

—. Theology. 1830-90. *75*

Translating and Interpreting. Jews. Michigan (Detroit). Rabbis. 1880-1959. *91*

Travel. Clergy. Montana. Presbyterian Church. Sunday schools. 1870's-1927. *68*

Trials. Episcopal Church, Protestant. Heresy. New York (Rochester). Reform. St. Andrew's Church. 1879-1927. *53*

Trinitarians. Calvinism. Unitarianism. 1780-1840. *45*

Tshimakain Indian Mission. Diaries. Frontier and Pioneer Life. Missions and Missionaries. Oregon (Forest Grove). Washington. 1833-97. *243*

U

Ukrainian Americans. *Alaska Herald.* Editors. Far Western States. Priests. 1832-1916. *93*

Union Theological Seminary. New York. Presbyterian Church. Schisms. Theology. 1865-70. *203*

Unionists. Civil War. Publishers and Publishing. Reconstruction. State Politics. Tennessee. 1825-77. *32*

Unitarianism. Calvinism. Trinitarians. 1780-1840. *45*

—. Clergy. Historians. Massachusetts (Beverly). Rhode Island. 1833-47. *215*

—. Lectures. Minnesota (Minneapolis). Norwegian Americans. 1881-82. *103*

—. Massachusetts. Orientalism. Transcendentalism. 1840's-82. *105*

Universalists. Clergy. Liberals. Missouri (St. Louis). Protestants. 1867-1923. *43*

Utah. Agricultural College of Utah, Logan. Brigham Young College. Colleges and Universities. Educational Administrators. Mormons. State Politics. 1894-1907. *110*

—. Bishops. Episcopal Church, Protestant. Mormons. Social Change. 1905-14. *212*

—. Charities. Mormon Relief Society (Social Services Department). 1919-29. *125*

—. Friendship. Mormons. 1829-68. *111*

—. Great Plains. Indian-White Relations. Mormons. New York, western. 1835-51. *257*

—. Leaders. Mormons. Women. 1804-87. *209*

—. Mining. Mormons. 1814-69. *181*

—. Mormons. 1840's-81. *245*

—. Mormons. 1846-1909. *82*

Utah (Salt Lake City). Converts. Mormons. Negroes. Slavery. 1844-76. *44*

—. Great Britain. Letters. Mormons. Polygamy. Women. 1885-96. *40*

—. Illinois (Nauvoo). Migration, Internal. Mormons. 1841-48. *260*

Utah, southern. Mormons. Photographers. 1877-1928. *4*

V_____

Values. Conference on Jewish Relations. Jews. Philosophy. 1880-1947. *48*

Vatican. Jesuits. Personal Narratives. World War II. 1942-45. *138*

Vermont. Catholic Church. Episcopal Church, Protestant. Rites and Ceremonies. 1832-68. *94*

—. Congregationalism. Converts. Family. Missions and Missionaries. 1789-1819. *20*

Vermont (Ryegate). Antislavery Sentiments. Clergy. Presbyterian Church, Reformed. 1785-1820. *142*

Virginia. Church of England. Clergy. 1743-52. *58*

Virginia, University of. College Teachers. Discrimination. Jews. Johns Hopkins University. 1841-77. *224*

Visions. Adventists. Fullmer, Bert E. 1916-29. *194*

W_____

Washington. Diaries. Frontier and Pioneer Life. Missions and Missionaries. Oregon (Forest Grove). Tshimakain Indian Mission. 1833-97. *243*

Washington (Seattle). Clergy. First Presbyterian Church.

Social Reform. 1880's-1920. *135*

—. Fundamentalism. Presbyterian Church. Social reform. 1900-40. *134*

Western States. Documents. Missions and Missionaries. 1850-72. *120*

Whig **(newspaper).** Editors and Editing. Temperance Movements. Tennessee. 1838-51. *31*

Whig Party. Louisiana. Methodist Episcopal Church. 1843-46. *253*

Wilberforce University. African Methodist Episcopal Church. Blacks. Clergy. College Presidents. Lutheran Church. 1830-93. *168*

Wilshire Boulevard Temple. California (Los Angeles). Judaism (Reform). Lawyers. Rabbis. 1895-1927. *211*

Wisconsin. Diaries. Minnesota, northern. Missionaries. 1833-49. *69*

—. Indian-White Relations. Methodist Church. Missions and Missionaries. 1793-1883. *33*

Wisconsin (Milwaukee). Congregationalists. Plymouth Church. Social Gospel. 1880-1915. *233*

Wisconsin (Voree). Michigan (Beaver Island). Mormons. Polygamy. 1830-55. *218*

Women. Alberta (Red Deer River area). Homesteaders.

Missionaries. Personal narratives. Saskatchewan. 1905-64. *30*

—. California (San Bernardino). Charities. Henrietta Hebrew Benevolent Society. Jews. 1870-91. *2*

—. California (San Francisco). Chinese Americans. Missions and Missionaries. Presbyterian Mission Home. 1869-1920. *38*

—. Catholic Church. Franciscan Sisters. Minnesota (Winona). St. Teresa, College of. 1903-54. *145*

—. Colorado, northeastern. Frontier and Pioneer Life. Methodist Episcopal Church (North, South). 1874-91. *175*

—. Educational Reformers. Jews. New York City. Social Reformers. 1880-1912. *184*

—. Educators. India. Methodist Church. Missionaries. Women's Home Missionary Society. 1865-1901. *231*

—. Friends, Society of. Friendship. Letters. Pennsylvania. 1778-79. *158*

—. Great Britain. Letters. Mormons. Polygamy. Utah (Salt Lake City). 1885-96. *40*

—. Leaders. Mormons. Utah. 1804-87. *209*

—. Mormons. Suffrage. ca 1870-1910. *248*

Women, status of. Mormons. 1830-90. *210*

Subject Index

Women's American Baptist Home Missionary Society. Baptists. Missions and Missionaries. Oklahoma (Wichita Mountains). 1893-1961. *54*

Women's Home Missionary Society. Educators. India. Methodist Church. Missionaries. Women. 1865-1901. *231*

Wood, James F. Catholic Church. Fenians. Ireland. Pennsylvania (Philadelphia). Speeches, Addresses, etc. 1839-75. *149*

World Alliance of Reformed Churches. Ecumenism. Evangelical and Reformed Church. Presbyterian Church. 1900-55. *182*

World War II. Jesuits. Personal Narratives. Vatican. 1942-45. *138*

Wyoming (Cheyenne). Congregationalism. Missions and Missionaries. Nationalism. Social Gospel. 1871-1916. *219*

Y_____

Yankton Reservation (Marty Mission). Catholic Church. Sioux Indians. South Dakota. 1918-49. *66*

Z_____

Zionism. Assimilation. Jews. 1914-40's. *148*

—. Judaism, Reform. Leadership. 1880-1929. *88*

—. New York City. 1900-12. *128*

AUTHOR INDEX

A

Abrams, Jeanne 213
Alexander, Jon 208
Allen, Richard 24
Alten, Diana 108
Anderson, Grant K. 92
Anderson, Philip J. 119
Andrews, William L. 61
Armstrong, Frederick H. 133
Ash, James L., Jr. 222
Ashdown, Paul G. 188

B

Baker, T. Lindsay 144
Baldassarre, Raffaele 9
Barnhart, Gordon 162
Bates, Irene M. 207
Beecher, Maureen Ursenbach 209
Benkart, Paula 73
Berrol, Selma 184
Bolt, Robert 192
Brackenridge, R. Douglas 26
Bradley, Martha 212
Bray, Robert 41
Bredin, Thomas F. 106
Brettell, Caroline B. 46
Briceland, Alan V. 137
Brown, Earl Kent 231
Brown, Violet 30
Burrus, Ernest J. 70
Buryk, Michael 93

C

Campbell, Debra 81
Cannon, Kenneth L., II 263
Canuteson, Richard L. 117
Chase, Theodore 254
Clapson, Clive 118

Clar, Reva 18 19 196 211
Clark, Michael D. 27
Clow, Richmond L. 50
Coates, Lawrence G. 257
Coleman, Louis 36
Collins, Patrick W. 247
Compton, Stephen C. 153
Conforti, Joseph 28 29 95
Conklin, Forrest 31
Cook, Lyndon W. 76
Cornwall, Rebecca 258
Coughlin, Robert C. 5
Cousins, Leone B. 179
Crawford, John R. 237
Cuba, Stanley L. 114
Curtis, Peter H. 107
Cuthbertson, B. C. 169

D

Davies, J. Kenneth 181
Davies, Phillips G. 57
Deibert, William E. 7
Dennison, Mary S. 127
Derge, John 233
Derounian, Kathryn Zabelle 158
Dickerson, Dennis C. 60
Dobbins, Gaines S. 42
Doraisamy, Theodore R. 161
Dosker, Nina Ellis 68
Draxten, Nina 103
Duchschere, Kevin A. 198
Dunlop, A. C. 1

E

Edwards, Paul M. 206
Ellenson, David 99
Emlen, Robert P. 55
Engerman, Jeanne 122
Engh, Michael E. 174

F

Farley, Benjamin W. 37
Feuer, Lewis S. 224
Fisher, Marcelia C. 235

Foote, Cheryl J. 23
Forness, Norman O. 220
Foster, Lawrence 228
Fowler, Arlen L. 10
Francis, Rell G. 4
Frank, Albert H. 154
Franklin, John Hope 249
Frazier, Arthur H. 197
Freeman, Olga 178

G

Geissler, Suzanne B. 34
George, Joseph, Jr. 149
Goff, James R., Jr. 167
Good, Donald G. 12 13
Greene, Dana 150
Gregory, Thomas J. 185
Grenz, Stanley J. 6
Gura, Philip F. 131 172 251

H

Hancock, Harold B. 146 147
Heath, Alden R. 62
Heath, William G., Jr. 11
Hefner, Loretta L. 124 125
Hench, John B. 234
Hennesey, James 138
Henry, Marcus H. 89
Hershman, Eiga 91
Hershman, Ruth 91
Hill, Marvin S. 204
Hinckley, Ted C. 102
Hiner, N. Ray 130
Hockman, Dan M. 58
Hoffmann, R. Joseph 75
Holder, Ray 252 253
Hoover, Roy 69
Hornbein, Marjorie 74
Horner, Patricia V. 243
Hoyt, Frederick B. 72
Huber, Donald L. 56

I

Ijams, Ethel W. 217

J

Jacobsen, Douglas 236
Janick, Herbert 187
Jeansonne, Glen 202
Jessee, Dean C. 259 260
Johnston, Patricia Condon 101
Jones, Charles T. 256

K

Kaganoff, Nathan M. 78
Kantowicz, Edward R. 152
Karier, Clarence J. 140
Kashatus, William C., III 165
Kelly, James C. 32
Kennelly, Karen 145
Killingsworth, Myrth Jimmie 205
Killoren, John J. 120
Kimball, Edward L. 112
Kimball, Stanley B. 111
King, Irving H. 200
Kintrea, Frank 170
Kirsch, George B. 15
Klein, Janice 64
Kolesnikoff, James D. 225
Kolesnikoff, Nina 225
Kramer, William M. 18 19 116
    196 211
Kreuter, Gretchen 145
Kring, Hilda Adam 77
Kristjanson, Wilhelm 229
Kydd, Ronald 221

L

LaFantasie, Glenn W. 250
LaFontaine, Charles V. 183 246
Leonard, Bill J. 155
Lewis, David Rich 218
Lieber, Constance L. 40
Lipscomb, Oscar H. 173
Loveland, Anne C. 87
Lovett, Robert W. 215
Luker, Ralph E. 63
Lyon, T. Edgar 126

M

Maclear, J. F. 98
Madsen, Carol Cornwall 248
Mappen, Marc 14
Margolies, Morris B. 238
Marshall, Mortimer Villiers 176
McClain, Laurene Wu 38
McCully, Bruce T. 156
McDade, Thomas M. 136
McGuffie, Duncan S. 45
McIlvenna, Don E. 110
McKernan, Mary 129
Meaney, Peter J. 25
Measures, Royce 159
Millar, W. P. J. 163
Miller, Char 20 21 22
Mondello, Salvatore 54
Moorman, Donald R. 261
Morgan, Edmund S. 171
Morris, Calvin S. 177
Mounger, Dwyn Mecklin 52
Mount, Graeme S. 100
Mount, Joan E. 100
Mueller, Roger C. 105
Mulder, John M. 121
Muller, Dorothea R. 219
Muller, Richard A. 203
Mullin, Robert Bruce 94
Mulvay, Jill C. 210
Murray, Andrew E. 139

N

Neuerburg, Norman 157
Noll, Mark A. 59 83 84 132
Noon, Thomas R. 168
Noonan, John T., Jr. 35
Nunis, Doyce B., Jr. 79 80

O

Oates, Stephen B. 113

P

Palmer, Richard F. 258

Papermaster, Isadore 166
Pauley, William E., Jr. 264
Peake, F. A. 3 97
Pearson, Daniel M. 223
Pearson, Fred Lamar, Jr. 8
Pearson, Samuel C., Jr. 43
Penner, Peter 242 244
Perin, Roberto 51
Peterson, Keith 190
Petryshyn, Jaroslav 201
Peyer, Bernd 160
Pies, Frank John, Sr. 16
Pies, Timothy Mark 16
Poe, William A. 85 86
Propst, Nell Brown 175
Pruyser, Paul W. 141

R

Richardson, Joe M. 143
Roeber, Anthony Gregg 49
Rogers, Tommy W. 232
Rollmann, Hans 186
Romig, Michael C. 182
Rosenfield, Leonora Cohen 48
Rosenthal, Jerome C. 128
Ross, Brian R. 96
Roth, Randolph A. 142
Rowley, Dennis 226
Russell, C. Allyn 134 199

S

Schmandt, Raymond H. 39
Schulte, Steven C. 33
Scult, Melvin 109
Sehr, Timothy J. 67
Shapiro, Herbert 214
Shipps, Jan 262
Siegel, Seymour 90
Silberger, Julius, Jr. 65
Sillito, John 212
Smith, Donald B. 71
Smith, George D. 189
Snyder, Marsha 240
Soden, Dale E. 135

Steele, Thomas J. 9
Stephens, Bruce M. 239
Stern, Norton B. 2 116 241
Stubblefield, Jerry M. 151
Stuhler, Barbara 145
Sutherland, John F. 115
Swanton, Carolyn 53
Sylvester, Lorna Lutes 180
Szasz, Ferenc M. 195 227

T_____

Thompson, Donald E. 180
Tomberlin, Joseph Aaron 8
Trotti, John Boone 255
Troy, Ferdinand M. 9
Tuchman, Barbara W. 148
Turner, Charles W. 230

V_____

VanHorne, John C. 164

W_____

Walker, Ronald W. 82
Waltmann, Henry G. 123
Watt, Ronald G. 245
Wax, Darold D. 110
Wechsler, Harold S. 104
Weeks, Louis 191
West, Ellis M. 47
White, Larry 194
Whyman, Henry C. 17
Williams, David 208
Winship, Win 193
Wolff, Gerald W. 66
Woods, Randall B. 216

Z_____

Zola, Gary P. 88
Zwerin, Kenneth C. 241

LIST OF PERIODICALS

Adventist Heritage

Alabama Review

Alaska Journal

Alberta History

American Benedictine Review

American Heritage

American Indian Quarterly

American Jewish Archives

American Jewish History

American Journal of Economics and Sociology

American Literature

American Quarterly

American West

American Presbyterians

Arizona and the West

Baptist History and Heritage

Baptist Quarterly

Beaver

Biography

Brigham Young University Studies

California Historical Quarterly

Canadian Ethnic Studies

Canadian Historical Review

Canadian Review of American Studies

Catholic Historical Review

Chronicles of Oklahoma

Church History

Collections of the Royal Nova Scotia Historical Society

Colorado College Studies

Commentary

Concordia Historical Institute Quarterly

Delaware History

Dialogue

Essex Institute Historical Collections

Fides et Historia

Filson Club History Quartelry

Foundations

Gateway Heritage

Georgia Historical Quarterly

Hawaiian Journal of History

Historical Journal of Western Massachusetts

Historical Magazine of the Protestant Episcopal Church

Historical New Hampshire

Historian

Idaho Yesterdays

Illinois Historical Journal

Indiana Magazine of History

Journal of American History

Journal of Canadian Studies

Journal of Ecumenical Studies

Journal of Mississippi History

Journal of Presbyterian History

Journal of Psychohistory

Journal of Religious Thought

Journal of the Canadian Church Historical Society

Journal of the History of Ideas

Journal of the Illinois State Historical Society

Jewish Social Studies

Journal of Psychohistory

Journal of the Early Republic

Journal of the West

Kansas History

Keystone Folklore

Louisiana History

Maryland Historical Magazine

Massachusetts Historical Society Proceedings

Massachusetts Review

Mennonite Life

Methodist History

167

List of Periodicals

Michigan History

Michigan Jewish History

Mid-America

Minnesota History

Missouri Historical Review

Missouri Historical Society Bulletin

Modern Age

Montana

Nebraska History

New England Historical and Genealogical Register

New England Quarterly

New Jersey History

New Mexico Historical Review

New-York Historical Society Quarterly

North Dakota History

North Louisiana Historical Association Journal

Norwegian-American Studies

Nova Scotia Historical Quarterly

Nova Scotia Historical Society Collections

Ontario History

Oregon Historical Quarterly

Pacific Historian

Pacific Northwest Quarterly

Palimpsest

Pennsylvania History

Pennsylvania Magazine of History and Biography

Polish American Studies

Proceedings of the American Antiquarian Society

Proceedings of the American Philosophical Society

Prologue

Quaker History

Records of the American Catholic Historical Society of Philadelphia

Rhode Island History

Rochester History

Saskatchewan History

Social History

South Carolina Historical Magazine

South Dakota History

South Dakota Historical Collections

Southern California Quarterly

Southern Studies

Studies in the American Renaissance

Swedish Pioneer Historical Quarterly

Swedish-American Historical Quarterly

Tennessee Historical Quarterly

Transactions of the Historical and Scientific Society of Manitoba

Transactions of the Moravian Historical Society

Transactions of the Unitarian Historical Society

Ukrainian Quarterly

Utah Historical Quarterly

Vermont History

Western Historical Quarterly

Western States Jewish History

William and Mary Quarterly

Wisconsin Magazine of History